KEEPING YOUR KIDS CATHOLIC

Keeping Your Kids Catholic

It May Seem Impossible But
It Can Be Done

Edited by Bert Ghezzi

Servant Publications
Ann Arbor, Michigan

Redeemer Books is an imprint of Servant Publications
especially designed to serve Roman Catholics.

Published by Servant Publications
P.O. Box 8617
Ann Arbor, Michigan 48107

Cover design by Michael Andaloro
Cover illustration by Gerry Gawronski

94 10 9 8 7

Printed in the United States of America
ISBN 0-89283-643-1

Library of Congress Cataloging-in-Publication Data

Keeping Your Kids Catholic : it may seem impossible but it
can be done / edited by Bert Ghezzi.
        p.   cm.
    "A Redemeer book."
    ISBN 0-89283-643-1
    1. Family—Religious life.   2. Christian education—
Home training.   3. Catholic Church—Education.
4. Christian education of children.   5. Christian
education of teenagers.   6. Christian education of young
people.   I. Ghezzi, Bert.
BX2351.K44   1989
248.8'45—dc20
                                        89-36677
                                          CIP

Also by Bert Ghezzi

Becoming More Like Jesus
Transforming Problems
The Angry Christian
Getting Free
Facing Your Feelings
Emotions as Resources (with Mark Kinzer)
Build With the Lord

Contents

FOUR / MAKING YOUR HOME CATHOLIC

FIVE / SHAPING KIDS CATHOLIC

SIX / KEEPING TEENAGERS CLOSE TO CHRIST

SEVEN / ROOTING KIDS IN
THE CATHOLIC HERITAGE

EIGHT / TRAINING KIDS
IN CATHOLIC MORALITY

NINE / COMMUNICATING A CATHOLIC
APPROACH TO THE WORLD

TEN / LOOKING BACK, LOOKING AHEAD

Acknowledgments

I want to thank Mary Lou, my wife, and my children, who with good humor put up with my telling Ghezzi family stories (though they claim I embroider them). Also I appreciate my editors: Ann Spangler, who for many years has graciously forced me to write better, and David Came, who worked hard with me to make this a better book. Thanks, too, to Marie Yasinskas of St. Leo College Library, St. Leo, Florida, who helped me track down articles and books, and to my friends, Debbie Viel and Linda Schwalbe, who very competently assisted in the preparation of the manuscript.

Contributors

*Thanks to the following who generously contributed to **Keeping Your Kids Catholic** by writing about their lives and by giving good advice:*

Jim Auer is a Catholic high school teacher. His articles appear frequently in the Catholic press and he is the author of seven books for teenagers, including *10 Steps to God: Spirituality for Teens* (Liguori). His family, including two teenagers, live in Cincinnati, Ohio.

Robert Bevans-Kerr has served as a counselor in youth drug rehabilitation programs and is currently the youth minister at St. Mary Magdalen Parish in Altamonte Springs, Florida. He and his wife Janece are parents of two small children.

John C. Blattner is editor of *Pastoral Renewal* and director of the Center for Pastoral Renewal, Ann Arbor, Michigan. John is author of several books, including *Growing in the Fruit of the Spirit* (Servant). John and his wife, Peggy, are raising four children.

Mark Berchem is the director of the St. Paul Catholic Youth Center, St. Paul, Minnesota, and the executive director of the National Evangelization Teams (NET). NET is a Catholic retreat ministry that ministers to teenagers in over fifty dioceses in the United States. Mark and Mary, his wife, have two daughters.

John J. Boucher is the executive director of Charism, an adult renewal and education center in the Diocese of Rockville Center, Long Island, New York. His wife, **Therese Boucher,** is a religious educator who has been involved in catechesis at every age level. Both have written many articles in the Catholic press, and Therese is the author of the book, *Becoming a Sensuous Catechist* (Twenty-Third Publications). They are raising their five children on Long Island, New York.

Tim Briffett is the director of REACH, an organization of young adults that evangelizes Catholic teens in the Northwest. He and his wife, Maralee, are raising their children in Yakima, Washington.

Barbara Burthoff is a nationally syndicated columnist, who writes regularly about making family life work well. She has been a newspaper writer for more than twenty years. She also teaches summer art classes for children.

Cindy Cavnar has written many articles about the saints, several of which appear in "Clouds of Witnesses," her regular column in *New Covenant.* She and her husband, Nick, live in Ann Arbor, Michigan, where they are caring for three kids they hope will grow up to be like the saints.

Therese Cirner and Randall, her husband, are raising their family as members of The Word of God, an interdenominational Christian community in Ann Arbor, Michigan. Together they are the authors of *Ten Weeks to a Better Marriage* (Servant), teach a seminar called "More for Your Marriage," and write a column on marriage and family in *New Covenant.*

Judy Cummings is a single parent and the mother of four teenage children. She is a computer specialist for EXXON in Houston, Texas, and has her own marketing business.

Dolores Curran is a parent, an internationally known lecturer, a nationally syndicated columnist, and the author of ten books. She won the Christopher Award for *Traits of a Healthy Family* (Harper & Row). Mrs. Curran has written for many years about handing on the faith to children.

Bill Dodds and his wife Monica are raising their three children in Mountlake Terrace, Washington. Bill is an award-winning journalist, and has recently published a family humor book titled *The Parents' Book of Dirty Tricks* (Meadowbrook Press).

Richard and Patricia Easton and their family of three children live in MacMurray, Pennsylvania. Richard is professor of English at Washington & Jefferson College, where he teaches creative writing. Patricia Harrison Easton is the author of two teen novels, *Summer's Chance* and *Rebel's Choice* (Harcourt, Brace, Jovanovich).

David Farmer and his wife Judy are raising their two sons in Ann Arbor, Michigan, where he works for a company that customizes van interiors. Formerly, David served as an editor at *New Covenant* magazine.

Mitch and Kathy Finley served five years as directors of the Family Life Office for the Diocese of Spokane, Washington. Together they wrote *Christian Families in the Real World* (Thomas More Press). They have three young sons, Sean, Patrick, and Kevin.

Karen Heffner is a registered nurse, college instructor, church volunteer, and free-lance writer. She and her husband of thirty-three years are parents of four adult daughters and they live in Freemont, California.

Robert Iatesta is president and co-founder of Families in Christ, a Catholic lay ministry dedicated to strengthening

Christian family life. He is a well-known speaker and author of *Fathers—A Fresh Start for the Christian Family* (Servant). He lives in Springfield, Pennsylvania, with Anna, his wife, and seven children.

Mary Ann Kuharski, a Minneapolis homemaker, is the mother of thirteen children, six of whom are adopted, handicapped, and of mixed races. She is a prolific writer whose articles appear frequently in the Catholic press.

Paul Lauer—former profligate, one-time Buddhist, born-again surfer—is now the editor of *Veritas* Catholic youth magazine. He is a young Catholic adult and is single, living in Los Angeles, California.

Jim Manney is the editor of *New Covenant* and the author of several books, including *Death in the Nursery* (Servant). He and his wife, Sue, have four children.

Patti Mansfield and her husband, Al, live in Metairie, Louisiana, with their family of four children. Both are internationally recognized leaders in the Catholic charismatic renewal. Patti writes "Notebook," a monthly column in *New Covenant,* and is the author of *Proclaim His Marvelous Deeds* (Franciscan University Press).

Connie Marshner is the author of *Decent Exposure: How to Teach Your Children About Sex* (Wolgemuth & Hyatt). She and her husband William, who teaches at Christendom College, live with their three children in Gaithersburg, Maryland.

Ralph Martin and Anne are the parents of six children. He has written many books including *A Crisis of Truth* and *Called to Holiness* (Servant). He serves as a leader of *FIRE,* a Catholic evangelistic alliance, and of The Sword of the Spirit, an international, ecumenical Christian community.

Joseph Moore is director of the religious studies department at Cardinal Spellman High School, Brockton, Massachusetts, and teaches youth ministry at St. Joseph College, West Hartford, Connecticut. He is the author of many books, including *When a Teenager Chooses You* (St. Anthony Messenger).

Thomas Nash is the seventh of Joseph and Genevieve Nash's family of eight, which they raised in southeastern Michigan. Tom has an M.A. in Journalism from the University of Missouri and is currently a free-lance journalist in Ann Arbor, Michigan.

Gertrud M. Nelson is a lecturer and illustrator, who lives in California with her husband and three children. Her most recent book is *To Dance with God* (Paulist).

William J. O'Malley, S.J., teaches theology and English at Fordham Preparatory School, Bronx, New York. Currently he is writing *Selling Faith to Skeptics*, a book about the evangelization of teenagers. He writes with the wisdom he has gleaned from twenty-three years of teaching teens.

Ralph F. Ranieri and his wife, Mary Liz, are raising their family in Ocala, Florida, where he practices as a licensed marriage and family life counselor. His articles appear regularly in the Catholic press.

Michael Schwartz is director of the Free Congress Center for Catholic Policy in Washington, D.C. He is the author of *The Pentecostal Prejudice* (Our Sunday Visitor). He and Rose Ann, his wife, are parents of four children.

Van and Janet Vandagriff are parents of seven adult Catholic children. Janet is a homemaker, professional grandmother, and conference speaker. In addition to keeping up with Janet, Van is president of Vandagriff Marketing Communications Services.

ONE

Keeping Kids Catholic

*With God's grace and a little help from friends, you
have a good start at raising your family Catholic.*

You Can Do It

*With the support of parish and friends, Catholic
parents can shoulder their responsibility to lead their
children to Christ.*

Bert Ghezzi

Just as I got back to the pew from distributing communion, our friend Elizabeth whispered in my ear with great
concern: "Oh, Bert, I promise that from now on I'll help Mary
Lou with the kids when you're giving out communion."
Whatever I missed, I thought, it must have been quite a
show.

"What on earth is going on?" I asked Mary Lou, my wife.

"You didn't see?" she said. I shrugged a no. "Well, Father
Lunsford gave Peter a host by mistake." Peter was then five
years old. "And he skipped back to the pew, waving it in the
air and shouting, 'I got one! I got one!' And then Clare (age
two) grabbed it from him."

"Where is it now?" I asked.

"I wrestled it from Clare and ate it," said Mary Lou.

"Well, not to worry," I said a tad irreverently, "I'm sure Jesus fled the host the moment Peter got hold of it."

Then I began to remember all those saints' lives where it is told that the host hovered over the head of a small child, too young to receive First Communion, because Jesus so much wanted to be with the little saint. Since I was sure Jesus wanted to be with my little Peter and I was equally sure that Peter was not yet a little saint, I thought that I might be getting some insight into the origin of some of those legends.

This is one of my favorite "war stories" from twenty-five years of working along with Mary Lou to raise our seven kids as good Catholics. Peter's unabashed desire to "get one" symbolizes the real openness of our kids to God. As they have grown older, I know that hunger is still there, but we have had a harder time showing our children how to satisfy it. Even though keeping our kids Catholic seems more difficult than ever, memories like this one encourage me, fill me with hope, and keep me laughing, which helps a lot.

I grew up in the church of the 1940s and 1950s, when raising kids Catholic was nearly automatic. All my widowed mother had to do to keep me Catholic was participate in St. Anne's Church, our parish in Castle Shannon, Pennsylvania. In those days local parishes were like factories that churned out Catholic kids. Catholic school, the priests and nuns, daily Mass, monthly confession, serving as an acolyte, and numerous other influences gave a uniquely Catholic shape to my young mind and heart. From ages six to eighteen, most of my friends were Catholic kids who were going through the same formation process. We became Catholics almost without having to think about it.

Times Have Changed. Today's Catholic parents are just as eager as my mother was to raise their children in the Christian faith, but they have a much harder time doing it. In the short thirty years since I graduated from Pittsburgh's St. Justin High School, a parish-supported school that like so many others exists no more, society and church have undergone revolutionary changes. As a result, several factors make it difficult for us to keep our kids Catholic. Consider just a few:

- Most parishes can no longer perform the function of fully catechizing and forming families and children as they once did.
- Many people are confused about what it means to be Catholic, and many Catholic parents are poorly informed about their faith.
- Like families everywhere, Catholic families are enduring increasing pressures. Many are struggling for survival, and deteriorating families have an especially hard time raising their kids Catholic.
- The lure of modern culture attracts kids more powerfully than family values and more persuasively than the influence of the church.

The situation is not a happy one. The sheer difficulty of raising our children as Christians can overwhelm us. We could pine for the good old days when the church seemed to do it for us, and we could get angry with our parishes for failing us. These would be mistaken responses, however, for they miss the advantages hidden in our problem. Challenging as they are, present circumstances provide us this great benefit: they have put responsibility for keeping kids Catholic back where it belongs—squarely on the shoulders of Catholic parents.

Of course, we need the aid of other Catholics in our parishes to help keep our kids Catholic. But in the past, Catholic parents too easily relied on the parish system to do what was really their job. The changes of the past quarter century are putting things back in balance. If there is now any hope that kids will grow up Christian, parents must take the lead, rather than expecting parishes to do it all for them.

But God Changes Hearts and Minds. We would be in deep trouble if introducing children to the faith depended exclusively on our efforts. The real work of winning young hearts and minds to Christ is God's, and no one desires their salvation more than God. Catholic parents are really God's partners in the task of keeping their kids Catholic. Here is another hidden benefit of the present circumstances. The challenge of leading children to Christ nudges parents themselves to turn to God. When Catholic parents begin to love God, they then have something to give their children.

Catholic parents are really God's partners in the task of keeping their kids Catholic.

Among the resources available to help parents raise their kids in the faith is the experience of others. Many Catholic families are grappling with the same issues and struggling with the same concerns. By grace, by trial and error, by hard work, and by imitating others, they have found ways of helping their kids embrace the Catholic faith.

Parents such as these, along with religious educators and youth ministers, write in *Keeping Your Kids Catholic* about what has worked for them. They speak not as "experts" who have all the answers, but as people like you and me, who love kids and are willing to try anything in order to bring them closer to Christ. Their willingness to speak candidly about their failures and successes in forming Catholic youth makes this a thoroughly practical book.

Here are some questions you probably wrestle with that writers address in these pages:

- How can I interest my kids in the Mass and the sacraments?
- How can I get our family to pray together?
- How can I teach my kids religion?
- How can I get my teenager to talk to me?
- How can I get my teenager to talk to God?
- Will I ever be able to get my family to study the Bible?
- How can I train my children in Catholic morality?
- What should I do about TV, teen music, and the youth culture?
- What if it doesn't work?

You will also find plenty of examples, and, as always, experience is the best teacher. The writers of *Keeping Your Kids Catholic* are good at "show and tell": they don't just tell you what to do, they show you what they did and how it worked. So among many such illustrations, you will read about:

- how different families learned to pray together as a family;
- how a family worships together at Mass;
- how one set of parents learned how to listen to their teenagers;
- how a mother takes opportunities to talk to her children about God;
- how a father turns discipline into a lesson about God's love and forgiveness;
- how one family has developed a support network of Catholic family friends.

And much more. The writers are realists. They recognize how hard it is to keep kids Catholic, but they are full of faith, since they know it's God's will to bring our sons and daughters to Christ. As a result, you will find here much good advice and encouragement, much help and hope. ■

How to Get the Most Out of This Book

Consult it as a resource,
use it to make a plan of action,
and study it with your friends.

Bert Ghezzi

Keeping Your Kids Catholic is for couples, single parents, pastors, teachers, religious educators, youth ministers—for anyone who has a concern for raising Catholic children. Writers have been sensitive to the various situations of different families. Single parents, for example, will find that with few exceptions they can effectively apply the advice given here.

Keeping Your Kids Catholic is a treasury of helps. You can dip in anywhere and find something useful. Scan the table of contents and something will surely catch your attention. You may get hooked on "Why Teens Stop Going to Mass," or you may wonder about the answer to "Can Parents Prevent Teen Drug Abuse?" You might want to plunge into subjects such as "Talking with Teens about Sex" or "What Kept Our Kids Catholic." You may even decide to start at the back and defuse your potential guilt feelings by reading "Is It Your Fault if Your Kids Leave the Church?" Wherever you begin, you are sure to find an article that speaks to your family's circumstances. You can use *Keeping Your Kids Catholic* as a handbook, a helpful resource to consult when you need it.

However, you might want to work through *Keeping Your Kids Catholic* more systematically. The book tries to cover all the major areas that will concern Catholic parents, although in most cases it offers a good running start rather than a comprehensive treatment. You can work your way through chapter by chapter, reflecting on your family's situation and making decisions that will help you bring your kids closer to Christ.

To help individuals, couples, or groups study the book, each chapter concludes with a guide called **Think, Pray, & Act,** which contains the following helps:

- You will find questions **For Reflection and Discussion,** which are designed to help readers grasp main points and understand the topic in a general way.

continued on next page

Tips for Study and Action

Here are some tips for those who decide to study the book as a tool for shaping their family. These suggestions can help you select planks for a simple strategy for keeping your kids Catholic:

1. Couples Must Agree on What to Do. A wife or husband who launches out on their own, without consulting their partner, will probably alienate their spouse. Instead of gaining, they may even lose ground in the family.

2. Make a Plan. As you work your way through the book, use the **Taking Stock** and **Plan for Action** at the end of each chapter to help you fashion your own plan. You can make the plan as comprehensive as you like, but stoutly resist the desire to implement it all at once.

3. Determine Your Priorities. Arrange the planks in your strategy in an order that reflects two concerns—what's important and what's possible. Remember that not everything is equally important and that sometimes you may be able to achieve what seems impossible.

4. Keep It Simple. To get started in your family, pick one or at most two simple practices. Anything more elaborate may

continued on next page

- **Taking Stock** will serve as a mirror to help you get a perspective on your family's situation in a specific area.
- **Plan for Action** helps you determine what steps you can take to introduce or strengthen a practice in your family. The aids guide you in tailoring an approach that will work for you.
- An **Activity** is suggested as a way of introducing an area to you or to your children. Often they are family fun events. Since children identify with what they enjoy, giving them pleasant faith experiences is an important part of raising them Catholic.

collapse under its own weight. Once you overcome inertia and have achieved a little momentum, you can slowly add new elements, preferably one at a time. When you add something new, be sure to continue what you started before.

5. Start with Something You Are Relatively Sure Will Work. A successful start will build your confidence, giving you the encouragement you will need for moving ahead.

6. Take Time to Explain Why. If your children are old enough to ask "why?" be sure to instruct them in the reasons for your family's Catholic practices. That's how they make the faith their own.

7. Consider the Ages and Experience of Your Kids. With younger children, you can gradually introduce a full program of Catholic life in your home.

If your children are already teenagers and have no previous experience of Catholic family practices, you will certainly have to settle for less. Try prayers before meals and brief, informal conversations about Catholic perspectives on current events. If you haven't already lost the battle, try worshiping together at Mass.

Bert Ghezzi

For Reflection and Discussion and **Resources** start at the end of this chapter. **Taking Stock** and **Plan for Action** begin at the close of chapter two. The first **Activity** is suggested at the conclusion of chapter four.

The Support Factor. Catholic families do a better job of raising their children in the faith if they have the support of other Catholic families. For this reason, you may choose to study *Keeping Your Kids Catholic* with other parents. A Renew group, a local chapter of the Christian Family Movement, or other organized small group could elect to work their way through the book. Or you could get together regularly with one or more families in your parish, preferably but not necessarily with children about the same age as yours. For conversation starters use the **For Reflection and Discussion, Taking Stock,** and **Plan for Action** segments at the end of each chapter. Group use of the book can provide opportunities for discussing efforts, understanding failures, refining attempts, and celebrating successes.

Groups of families who want to work together through *Keeping Your Kids Catholic* may choose to use the following simple format:

1. Meet for one hour and a half each month. Select a day and time when everyone can come for about twelve consecutive months. The first session can be a time for planning what the group will do.

2. Meet in different homes each time. The host couple or parent should act for the evening as convener and discussion leader. Baby-sitting needs may require meeting at the same home each time. Even if that's the case, you can still rotate leadership.

3. The following schedule is suggested, but it may be adapted as needed:

- Five minutes—Opening prayer and brief Scripture reading;

- Twenty-Five minutes—Discussion, using **For Reflection and Discussion**;
- Twenty-Five minutes—Sharing about each family and getting help from each other, possibly using **Taking Stock** and/or **Plan for Action**;
- Ten minutes—Prayer aloud together for specific family needs;
- Twenty-Five minutes—informal time, including refreshments if desired;

4. Couples and single parents alike should be included.

5. Remember that everything discussed should be held in confidence, so that real openness and accountability are possible.

6. If groups choose, they could share about the following questions each month:

a. Have I been faithful in praying for my family?
b. Have we kept our commitment to family prayer times?
c. What are we working on this month? Has it been a success or failure so far?
d. What advice does the group have for me?

7. Begin the first week with a discussion of the next article in this chapter, "Who, Me, Teach My Child Religion?" by Dolores Curran. Use **For Reflection and Discussion** at the end of the chapter.

Remember that well-known, wide, and spacious road which is lavishly paved with good intentions? Take the narrower, more rugged path, and once you have thought it through a little, act on your decisions. Don't just stand there. Do *something* to keep your kids Catholic and draw them closer to Christ. ■

Who, Me, Teach
My Child Religion?

*Teaching religion is parent's business, and must begin
in the home, just like teaching health, safety, manners,
compassion, fairness, and all the other subjects
parents weave into that grand lesson called "life."*

Dolores Curran

We don't feel confident in our ability to teach our children religion because until recently we weren't expected to be competent. The unspoken conclusion was that the church taught religion because parents couldn't. We got the subtle message: "You can't teach your children religion, so don't try." Now we're sincerely trying to break that cycle by teaching parents that they *must* teach religion in their home and that children *can* learn it and enjoy it if we expect them to.

We don't have to worry about expecting too much. There's a difference between expectation and pressure. If children sense that we expect them to achieve, they will give their all. Pressure comes when we don't expect them to learn while insisting they do. "I don't care if it takes all year, you're going to learn this" is an example of pressure. "This is tricky but you won't have any trouble learning it" is expectation.

You Can Teach Your Children Religion. We are successful teachers in many subjects, possibly because we don't realize we are teaching. We accept this parental teaching casually. It is part of our job and can be a very rewarding experience.

But we draw a block at teaching religion. Why? Because it's new, so fraught with old catechism memories that we aren't relaxed about it.

How do our children learn personal cleanliness? Not through the few formal health units they encounter at school. These are helpful but they generally come *after* the child has learned informal lessons at home. We use every daily opportunity to teach personal cleanliness. When our three-year-old boy drops his gumball at the supermarket, we don't wait until Saturday morning's sanitation class to explain that it's unsanitary to chew it. We stop shopping, dispose of the gum, and explain to the child then and there that the floor is dirty, that there are probably germs on the gum and that he might become ill from chewing it.

The gum loss is an incident but his inevitable question, "What's germs?" leads us into the actual lesson. On his level, we must effectively translate our adult knowledge of microbiology into his understanding. And we do it. The fact that we do it doesn't shock anyone. Teaching good health habits is one of the accepted parental functions. In fact, if a parent neglects this education, he's in for some of society's censure.

But what happens if the three-year-old wanders away, finds the gum counter, opens a pack, and happily returns to the cart smelling of peppermint? This is the incident which catapults us into religious education on the spot. Do we handle it the same way?

Do we understand that to the child this is as innocent as dropping the gum? Do we then explain that the gum isn't ours, that it must be paid for, and that someone might suffer as a result of our action? And when the child asks, "Whose is it and why can't I take it 'cause there's lots there for everybody?' " do we take the time to effectively translate our adult knowledge of morality and personal property into his three-year-old understanding?

Or do we spank his hands and tell him it's naughty?

The most effective deterrent to accepting our natural role as religious educators is a psychological one. Because our immigrant ancestors turned the job over to the church, the church unintentionally came to implant the idea that parents were incapable. And we believed it. We forget that the reason for abandoning such formation in the home has long since vanished.

We've Changed. We aren't an immigrant people today, fearful that new and strange cultures will strip the faith from our kids. We are, rather, an intelligent, educated people very much in tune with today's society. We find ourselves often in the paradoxical situation of discovering that the church is as incapable of teaching our children religion for today as our great-grandparents were yesterday.

Besides, it's very clear today that *we* are the church. The pastor isn't the church, the nuns aren't the church, even the bishop isn't the church. We all make up the church. So when we charge the church with failure, we are charging ourselves.

Who Is the Church? Isn't it time to set aside our old attitude of "the church, *it*," in favor of "the church, *we*"? Our first lesson as religious educators is to come to believe that we really are the church. Once we accept "we the church" as freely as we do "we Catholics," we can feel like genuine cooperative partners in our religious education efforts.

"Who, me? Teach my kids religion? Not until the church says I have to."

But who is the church? We are. Then we must change our answer to, "Not until *we* say we have to."

"Who, me? An engineer heading up thirty-two people?"

"Who, me? An ex-teacher?"

"Who, me? A wife who has taught herself to knit, balance the budget, and rear children?"

"Who, me? I'm just a parent."

We need to look at ourselves, study our children, and plunge in with a little humor, more hope, and a great deal of grace. We have the ability and desire. We lack the confidence. But if we in the church have succeeded in destroying our confidence, we can succeed in rebuilding it.

Our first lesson as religious educators is to come to believe that we really are the church.

Let's begin by understanding that our ancestors, far less talented and educated than most of us, accepted the challenge just as they accepted that of teaching their children plowing or cooking. They didn't make a big thing out of it. It was an integral part of their lives. They didn't go into nervous spasms at the thought of teaching their children religion. They merely put aside the pea shelling and whittling, and then began teaching. Are we willing to admit that we, living in this country in this age with all our resources, cannot do what they did?

"Who, me?"

Who else? ∎

Think, Pray, & Act

TEACHING KIDS THE FAITH

FOR REFLECTION AND DISCUSSION

1. What obstacles do parents face in deciding to introduce their kids to the faith?
2. How can we grow in confidence in teaching our kids religion?
3. Who has the greater responsibility in keeping kids Catholic—the church or the parents? Why?

Starting at the close of chapter two, you will find a variety of other exercises and activities designed to help you apply the advice and teaching of this book in your own family. Keep an eye out for the following headings at the end of future chapters:

> **Taking Stock**
> **Plan for Action**
> **Activity**

RESOURCES

The Catholic Family Reference Shelf. Every Catholic family should have access to a variety of books and other materials that will help them grow in faith. Families will value different books, but there are a few which every family ought to consider acquiring when they can afford them. Not everyone will agree with my recommendations, but this is the reference shelf of basic Catholic books that I suggest:

- *The New American Bible* (with Revised New Testament). Catholic Bible Press publishes an inexpensive paperback version of this translation authorized by the United States Catholic bishops.
- *The New St. Joseph Sunday Missal and Hymnal* is an affordable guide to Sunday Mass (Catholic Book Publishing Company).
- Alan Shreck, *Basics of the Faith: A Catholic Catechism* (Servant) is a good fundamental explanation of Catholic beliefs.
- The *Catholic Almanac,* (for the current year) by Felician A. Foy and Rose M. Avato and published by Our Sunday Visitor, provides an annual compendium of information about the Catholic church.
- *Vatican Council II: The Conciliar and Post Conciliar Documents,* Volume One, edited by Austin Flannery, O.P. (Liturgical Press), is the first place to look for the church's perspective on every facet of modern Christian living.
- *Handbook for Today's Catholic: Beliefs, Practices, Prayers* (Liguori) offers a brief introduction to the Catholic faith.

TWO

Why Kids Leave the Catholic Church

Understanding why young Catholics drop out of the Catholic church can give us insight into our own children's spiritual condition.

Why Teens Stop Going to Mass

Parents suspect that when their child gives up religious practice, the child has lost faith in God. It's not that simple.

William J. O'Malley, S.J.

Parents suspect that when their child gives up religious practice, the child has lost faith in God. It's not that simple.

First, Mass attendance is an external act. So guessing another's motives for attending—or not—is just that: guessing.

Second, after twenty-three years of teaching theology to about 3,000 high school and college students, I suspect that a teenager's dropping Mass may not always indicate loss of faith in God—for the simple reason that most teenagers have never actually made a real act of faith in God. Perhaps an act of faith in their parents' faith, or sister's faith, or "Everybody believes in God," but not their own personal realization of and personal commitment to God.

All the religion courses and homilies in the world will remain as cold as calculus unless one has a commitment to the person religion is all about.

In essence, we are asking our young to go to a weekly (and rather dull) testimonial dinner for a person they have never really met and certainly feel no need for. We will never begin to solve the problem of Mass and teenagers until parents, priests, and religious educators all bow to the truth that we are dealing with young people who are baptized but unconverted.

A Personal Relationship with God. The real answer, I think, lies in bringing youngsters to a personal relationship with God. All the religion courses and homilies in the world will remain as cold as calculus unless one has a commitment to the person religion is all about. And that faith commitment is a calculated risk. The schools can supply the data, the calculation part, but the individual student is the only one who can supply the risk.

But just as adults judge teenagers' motives, teenagers do the same of adults' motives. If parents' attendance at Mass seems to be a perfunctory and joyless fulfillment of form, if God is never spoken of in the home as a person with whom the parents have a real personal relationship, the teenager assumes that, even for the parents, the forty-five minutes on Sunday is at worst phony and at best deadened formalism.

Perhaps the parent does pray daily, perhaps he or she does have a true relationship with God. But I wonder in how many homes a parent ever talks about it. Parents talk plentifully of their business and social relationships, but in my experience they rarely speak of their divine relationship. How many parents ever tell their children how they came to meet the living God? Unless that happens, religion for the teenager remains something unreal, to be endured a few classes a week and once on Sunday, until he or she gets sprung.

What, Then, Are We to Do? Religious education—in school, at home, in church—should focus on fostering a personal relationship between the teenager and God, particularly by elders honestly sharing with their young their own relationship with God. One ordinarily does not achieve a friendship with a person, divine or human, by having a debate about him with a third party—although far too many religion classes and family discussions end up that way. One gets to know and love a person by acknowledging his presence, being with him a lot, sharing. But how many parents or pastors or teachers talk openly to teenagers about their own prayer life: how to begin praying, how often they do it, what kinds of things they say, what it means to them? Why should teenagers try to know God better when they have no knowledge that their parents know God at all?

Making the God of the textbooks real is not just one of the aims of religious education; it is *the* aim. All talk of the church is mere historical curiosity; all talk of morality is mere ethical debate; all talk of liturgical innovation is merely formalism dressed up in new clothes—unless one has met God, cares about God or, at the very least, feels grateful to God. ■

Are We Reaching Our Youth?

*Young Catholics are looking for
God's personal love, not an external faith.*

Mark Berchem

For too long we have been trying to pass on an external faith to young people. We tell them stories about Christ and instruct them in doctrine so they will know what to believe. We expect them to live according to God's commandments, which we teach them by word and example.

We hope to attract them to this faith by involving them in religious activities, but it doesn't seem to be working. Young people today do not need more things to do. Religious activities compete with school, extracurriculars, jobs, friends and so on, and, quite frankly, almost always lose out.

The Search for Meaning Continues. While many young people have abandoned the church, they have not abandoned their search for meaning. Everyone longs to find something or someone that can fill the emptiness they feel within. Much of what young people do today can be understood as their own search for this fulfillment. They are suffering from loneliness, from hopelessness, from consumerism, from drug and alcohol abuse, from sexual immorality, and from secularism. They suffer because the gods which our society worship and hold up to them do nothing to satisfy their deep needs.

What young people are searching for—in fact what all of us are searching for—is a personal relationship with Jesus Christ. Christ and Christ alone can fill the emptiness they feel so keenly. They not only need to hear that Jesus loves them, they need to experience his love for themselves. They not only need to hear what Christ did in the Gospels, they need to see what Christ can do today in their own lives.

Young people need an internal faith—a faith that burns from within, a faith that says I believe not because I was told to believe, but because I have seen for myself. This internal faith comes not from knowing about Christ, but from knowing Christ. Consider the beautiful scene in the movie "Jesus of Nazareth" when Mary Magdalene brings the apostles the good news that Jesus had risen from the dead. Faced with their disbelief and doubt, she says, "I know he is alive. I have seen him for myself." If our faith is going to be passed on to the next generation, then, like Mary Magdalene, our kids must meet Christ personally.

What can we do to help this next generation of Catholics meet Christ?

We can start by witnessing to the vitality of our own faith. We must catch our kids' attention by how we live. Does our faith make any difference to us? Ask yourself:

- Do I pray every day?
- Do I read the Bible regularly?
- Are my values shaped by the Word of God or by television series and opinion polls?
- Do I receive the body and blood of Christ in the Eucharist?
- Do I pray with my family?
- Do I speak out against things I know are wrong, even though others may disagree?
- Do I speak about my faith with my son or daughter, my friends and neighbors?

How we live our faith really does make an impression on our children. Who do you think kids are looking at? It's ordinary me and ordinary you. They see us day in and day out in real life situations. We can show them that Christ is alive and that our faith really does make a difference. ◼

Why Young Catholics Leave, and What Parents Can Do to Prevent It

*Studies of young dropouts suggest
ways parents can draw their kids to God.*

Bert Ghezzi

An estimated 42 percent of all Catholics leave the church at some time during their lives.[1] At present more than 50 percent of those dropping out are young Catholics, twenty-five years of age or younger.[2] Not very encouraging statistics, especially for parents.

However, the same sociologists who gave us the numbers have also been able to pin down the main reasons kids leave the church. Grappling with these factors may suggest some strategies parents could use to keep their own children close to Christ and the church.

In *Converts, Dropouts, Returnees*, Dean R. Hoge classifies young Catholic dropouts into three main categories: family-tension dropouts, weary dropouts, and lifestyle dropouts (see chart on the next page).

More than half of young dropouts are in the *family-tension* category. These young persons experience pressure or problems in their family, and at the first chance rebel against their parents and the church. They usually drop out as soon as they leave home, or when parents relax the pressure.

Hoge says that this rebellion against parents takes two forms:

In one type of situation these young persons have received religious education and have attended Mass during childhood and early adolescence yet for various

Types of Young Catholic Dropouts*	
	Percent of Dropouts 22 Years Old & Under
1. *Family-tension Dropouts*	52
2. *Weary Dropouts*	23
3. *Lifestyle Dropouts*	19
4. *Spiritual-need Dropouts*	2

* Based on Table 6.1, in Dean R. Hoge, *Converts, Dropouts, Returnees* (New York: The Pilgrim Press, 1981), p. 96.

reasons have never internalized or "owned" their faith. They do not identify with the faith or with the Catholic church. As they grow older, they feel no motivation to go to church, and as soon as family pressure is off, they drop out . . .

The other form comprises a general rebellion by the youth against their families and all their families stand for. This situation is laden with emotion; when one talks with the youth one hears long histories of bad feelings, most of which are unrelated to churchgoing or religion. The youths may charge the church with faults and weaknesses, but these charges are not explanations for their behavior; they are rationalizations.[3]

Weary or "bored" dropouts are persons who no longer have any motivation for attending church, and a large number of young Catholics who leave fit this description. They usually give some recent external event as a reason for their leaving, such as a job change or a conflict with their pastor, but the deeper reason is internal. Hoge says of weary dropouts: "An inner faith and spiritual life is lacking, hence motivation is weak."[4]

Another large group of young Catholics leave the church

because their *lifestyle* conflicts with church teaching. Usually their difficulties stem from moral problems in the area of sex, such as masturbation, homosexual activity, premarital sex, or cohabitation. Faced with the option of changing their behavior or leaving the church, they drop out. Even if these young Catholics have internalized their faith—and it can be safely assumed that most have not—their religious commitment is no match for their sexual activity or relationships.

What lessons can parents learn from these sociological studies? There are significant clues that could lead to strategies for keeping our kids Catholic.

Lesson 1: Resolve Family Problems. Fifty-two percent of young Catholics drop out not because they have problems with the church, but because they are rebelling against their parents. Church attendance becomes a weapon in family warfare, a way for a young person to set himself against his mom and dad.

Parents should put emphasis on making family relationships positive for every member. Good communication is essential, as is the determination to deal with problems as they arise, so that they don't hang around and reproduce, hatching a whole brood of new problems.

Good family life does not guarantee that a child will not leave the church. However, eliminating as much family tension as possible removes circumstances that prompt kids to drop out.

Lesson 2: Help Young Catholics Develop a Personal Relationship with God. Young Catholic dropouts fall into different categories, but their underlying condition is the same. They have not "internalized" their faith, they are limited to "externals," they do not "own" their Catholic religion, they don't "identify" with the Catholic church, they have no "intrinsic motivation," "inner faith," or "spiritual life." The common denominator here is that young dropouts do not know God personally. And not knowing him, they cannot love him.

Meeting God affects people—it motivates them. It gives their life meaning; it even persuades them to behave morally. So what can we do to help our kids come to know God? The following could be planks in our strategy:

- Parents must come to know and love God above all. Prayer, Scripture study, talking with priests and lay leaders, involvement in renewal movements—all are avenues we should pursue.

- We should make God present in our homes through family prayer and by speaking to our children about our relationship with him.

- We should teach Catholic

- Parents should link their kids up with young Catholic adults, just a little older than they, who are serious about God and about their faith. Children often listen to mentors who are closer to them in age.

continued on next page

Sounding Boards

Studies show that most children eventually return to the religious values with which they were raised. They may drift, they may do this in a rebellious way. The best thing adults can do is to be good sounding boards and listen to their doubts and concerns. We also can be patient with their alienation and not take it personally. Most important, we can pray for them.

Joseph Moore

You get the idea. Do whatever you can to help the kids experience God personally.

Lesson 3: Pray. Sociological surveys and practical advice that we find summed up in articles like this may give us a false sense of control. Just complete these three easy steps... Or more likely, they may give us a headache, overwhelming us with the difficulty of the job.

The reality is that we must do whatever we can, no matter how puny it may seem, and trust God to accomplish the goal of saving our children. So the best and most effective plank in our plan must be prayer.

Jesus promised repeatedly to grant any request we make in his name. In other words, when we pray according to his will, we can be sure our prayer will be answered. What could be more in line with his will than bringing our children to know, love, and serve God and to live with him forever? So let's keep on expecting God to keep our kids Catholic and Christian, or to bring them back to him, if they have dropped out. ◼

Notes

1. "Church Dropouts: Changing Patterns of Disengagement and Re-entry," *Review of Religious Research*, 21:427-50 (1980).
2. Dean Hoge et. al., *Converts, Dropouts, Returnees: A Study of Religious Change Among Catholics* (New York: The Pilgrim Press, 1981), p. 82.
3. Hoge, p. 97.
4. Hoge, p. 105.

Think, Pray, & Act

EVALUATING AND PRAYING FOR YOUR FAMILY

FOR REFLECTION AND DISCUSSION

1. Why do young people stop attending Mass? How do parents affect this choice? (See article by O'Malley.)
2. What must parents do to reach their kids? (See articles by O'Malley and Berchem.)
3. What are the reasons young people leave the church? (See article by Ghezzi.)
4. What can parents do to help prevent their kids from leaving the church? (See articles by Berchem and Ghezzi.)

TAKING STOCK

To get the most out of this feature, consider keeping a notebook.

Spend a few minutes thinking about each child in your family. How would you describe the child's relationship with God? How does the child relate to the church?

PLAN FOR ACTION

Keeping a planning notebook may help you hold yourself accountable for things you would like to do.

Daily Prayer for Your Family. If you are not already praying each day for every member of your family, start today. The following suggestions will help you:

- Set aside five minutes to intercede for your family.
- Do it at the same time every day.
- If possible, find a place where you feel comfortable praying and spend your five minutes there each day.
- Spend a moment telling God you love him and thanking him for all he has done for you.
- Think of each family member, thank God for them, and pray for their relationship with God and for their specific needs.
- You may want to close your prayer time with an Our Father, Hail Mary, and Glory Be.

RESOURCES

For further and more detailed study on young dropouts and the attitudes of Catholic young people, consult the following:

- Dean R. Hoge, *Converts, Dropouts, Returnees* (New York: The Pilgrim Press, 1981).
- George Gallup, Jr., and Jim Castelli, *The American Catholic People* (Garden City, New York: Doubleday & Company, Inc., 1987).
- Joan L. Fee, Andrew M. Greeley, William C. McCready, and Teresa A. Sullivan, *Young Catholics: A Report to the Knights of Columbus* (New York: Sadlier, © 1981).

THREE

Keeping Parents Catholic

Kids may be the last to admit it, but parents exert a significant influence on the shape and direction of their children's lives. Parents must set the right example, and take a deliberate approach to handing on the faith to them.

As Parents Go, So Go the Kids

Our actions always speak louder than our words.

Bill Dodds

Being a parent would be a snap if my kids would just do what I say.

And quit watching me.

There isn't much chance of that. My wife Monica and I have three children, boys eight and thirteen and a girl eleven, and it's like living with three video cameras.

Worse.

Three Rich Littles, master impressionists ready to imitate anything we say or do, think or feel.

Take manners, for example. The other night we were sitting down to a lovely chicken dinner Monica had prepared and after we said grace, I snatched up a piece and started chomping away.

"When chicken is fixed this way," Monica was saying to the kids and paying no attention to me, "it's eaten with a knife and fork. It's not like the colonel just threw it into a bucket and you can reach right in and . . ."

But they weren't listening to her, they were staring at me.

"I need another napkin," I said. "I, uh, wanted to show you what NOT to do."

They didn't buy it.

"Don't do what I do." I think every parent feels that way. Often. They would like their children to know that rule number one is: "Don't do what I do."

Parents should never forget that no child follows rule number one.

What I Want My Children to Be, I Must Try to Be. I don't think there's any other way. Believe me, I've looked.

I spent a good deal of my childhood sneaking around, hoping my parents wouldn't see me.

They did.

And a good deal of my parenthood sneaking around, hoping my children wouldn't see me.

They did.

But it isn't just the not-so-great things that I tend to keep hidden. It's good things, too, and that's a mistake. The best parents come right out and show their children what they think and feel and believe.

Just thinking "I love you" is nothing like telling my son or daughter "I love you."

Ah, but he knows it, I can rationalize.

She knows I love her. Of course, I do.

He knows I'm proud of him.

She knows I think she's pretty.

Maybe. But there's nothing like hearing it. Flat out.

Saying "I love you" right out loud sends a double message. It says I love you and, it says it's all right to express affection to each other. It's more than just "all right." It's a very important thing.

Sharing the Faith with My Kids. My Catholic faith is also very important to me. It's a gift my parents gave to me and one I want to pass on to my children. I want them to know that God loves them unconditionally. I want them to come closer

---

Does "Catholic" mean Sunday morning or does it mean every day?

---

to him through the sacraments. I want them to know him personally. I want them to realize the church offers honest and consoling answers to so many of the questions they'll inevitably face.

Why was I created?

What am I supposed to do with my life?

What will make me truly happy, truly at peace?

Why do those I love have to die?

What happens to you when you die?

Kids today have a tougher time really believing any of this religion "jazz," because they are constantly bombarded by a consumer society that snickers at the idea of religion.

Society tells them that faith in God is antiquated. It's as cute, meaningless, and out of step with reality as a "Father Knows Best" rerun.

Earn a lot of money, society teaches them, and you will be happy.

Be famous, no matter what it takes.

Do whatever feels good, whenever it feels good.

There is no right or wrong.

And I'm supposed to combat that with just one hour per week at Sunday Mass?

No way.

I'm teaching my children religion when I tell the woman at the checkout stand that she has given me too much change.

When I refuse to laugh politely when an acquaintance tells a racist or sexist joke.

When I slow down to let another car pull in ahead of me on a busy street.

When I say "please" and "thank you" to their mother.

I don't have many recollections of my mother and father at Sunday Mass. They took us every week, but mostly I remember being told to shush and move away from my brother when I was little and being bored when I was older.

Our oldest child is getting to the age where he complains of Mass being boring. I agree with him. It is very boring compared to playing the latest video game or watching a car-chase scene in a good movie or speeding down the block on a bike. But kids need to learn that prayer, like friendship and love, isn't always action-packed, nonstop excitement.

It takes more work.

And it's more rewarding.

Parenting: A Twenty-Four-Hour-a-Day Job. My parents didn't teach me about being a Catholic during one hour on Sunday. It was during the other 167 hours of the week.

Once when I was ten or eleven, I went with my dad down to his office one Saturday afternoon. The building was locked and a security guard let us in. Dad stopped for a little while—it couldn't have been more than two or three minutes—and visited with the worker. Then he went on up and got whatever it was he needed to get.

I don't remember that part. I just remember him taking the time to be courteous. It was a simple lesson in treating other people with respect—a powerful lesson I'm sure dad doesn't remember giving. It was an unforgettable lesson for me.

I think about that more often as my own kids get older. What are my actions saying to them? What are the lessons they will never forget?

A father has a critical role in helping his children learn about the faith, even though he might not be the one to show his son the left shoulder is touched before the right shoulder when making the Sign of the Cross; even though he might not be the one to help his daughter review a homework assignment for a religious education class.

If you're a father (or a mother, for that matter), your children are watching.

If you're a Catholic father, they're watching to see just how serious this church business really is. Does "Catholic" mean Sunday morning or does it mean every day?

If you want your children to grow in the faith, it has to be every day.

I saw how my parents acted toward other people, toward us kids, toward each other, and I wanted to act the same way. Day by day they showed us what they considered valuable.

Where their treasure lies.

Where their hearts are.

All this sounds pretty lofty. Forgive me. If you're a parent, you know there's nothing more down-to-earth than raising kids. This also sounds like I know all the answers. Of course, I do. Every parent does. The problem is remembering them when the need arises. And it arises every day.

I would like to think teaching my children about the church has mostly to do with things like learning how to make the Sign of the Cross. Unfortunately, it has more to do with learning to live the cross.

Serving God.

Using one's talents.

Going last.

I think the best way for me to keep my kids Catholic is for me to stay—or become—a true practicing Catholic. But even then, there are no guarantees. Faith is a gift from God.

Raising my children to love God is something I have entrusted to the all-knowing God my parents introduced to me. I don't know a better way to repay them or thank him, than to try to help my own children see him, welcome him, into their own lives. ■

Why I am a Catholic Today

My parents did not talk about Catholicism.
They lived it joyously, even when it was hard.

Thomas J. Nash

My parents gave faithful and joyous witness to the Catholicism they wished to inspire in their eight children. I believe this is the major reason that I, a single Catholic at age twenty-seven, zealously strive to embrace the faith today.

Mom and Dad understood that they couldn't expect their kids to embody a religious system—a way of living—that they themselves did not believe and live. Their example prepared me to maintain my faith after I left home.

My parents did not just talk about the Catholic church as the church Christ founded almost two thousand years ago. And they didn't just talk about the many spiritual benefits the church offered, such as the sacraments, the rosary, the Bible, and so on.

They joyfully embraced the teachings of the church and enjoyed its rich offerings. As one priest-author says, they abandoned themselves to Divine Providence and reaped the wonderful spiritual harvest that comes with experiencing the fullness of Christianity.

My Parent's Example. I don't mean to imply that my parents are perfect or that they are not sinners. But mother and father believed their kids could understand and accept the fact that their parents would sometimes fail and have to repent. However, they also knew that they would undermine the likelihood of their children remaining lifelong Catholics if they as parents consciously and willfully disobeyed church teachings and disciplines.

So in both word and deed my parents gave a good and attractive witness to Catholicism:

- In their openness to having children, viewing offspring as a far greater blessing than the biggest house, car, cottage, boat, or vacation they could imagine.
- In the love they expressed to one another, and the stability and peace they brought to the household through their refusal to harbor grudges or bitterness against one another or their children. If ever there were a conflict at home, my parents reconciled quickly, as Christ taught.
- In my father's keeping his priorities in order, declining opportunities for promotion if these would diminish the time he could spend with the family.
- In my mother's patience in bad times, such as the time she had to go to the police station at 2:30 in the morning and pick up her bright son, Tom, who had been driving around with friends, spraying people with water from a fire extinguisher.
- In their recognition that the youngest of their children, Mary, who has Down's Syndrome, is indeed a great gift from God, not a burden. Mary has required more care than her elder siblings, but her love and joy for life has enriched us all.
- In their total and unconditional commitment to each other and their children, seeing their other seven kids

through Catholic schools and college and living a marriage which will soon celebrate its fortieth year.

- In their acknowledging that there would be trials—"Good Fridays"—in life, but adding that if we stayed close to Christ he would see us through to "Easter Sundays," where we would emerge as spiritually stronger persons. My parents introduced me to Jesus Christ as a person—my God and friend whom I should seek in everything I do.

I try to apply all that I've learned, hoping one day to expand my witness through radio/TV apologetics and evangelism. For now I strive to live a disciplined Christian life, supported by daily Mass, praying the rosary, and Bible study. I want to influence others for Christ personally and professionally. I look forward to the day when I am a husband and father and when, with my wife, I can build a Christ-centered home in which the Catholic faith is taught and celebrated. ■

Single Parents Have SPIRIT

This single mother faces the challenges of raising her kids for Christ with faith and determination.

Judy Cummings

Shortly after my divorce twelve years ago, I attended a Catholic singles seminar where one lady raised her hand and asked "How can I raise my kids Catholic, when my own head is all screwed up?" I listened to that question because I felt the same way. I was suffering from guilt, bitterness toward my ex-husband (actually, borderline hate), in-security, sub-poverty, and alienation from my church. Add to these negative situations a certain amount of insecurity about my future sex life and I was a mess. I needed help, not only for me, but for my children—help that could only come from God. But he also seemed to have abandoned me. Or possibly I had abandoned him.

Here I was, twenty-eight years old, four kids from newborn to six years old, no job, no child support—and scared. I had been raised as one of six children in a very Catholic home: Mass at 9:00 every Sunday morning, roast and potatoes for Sunday dinner, no divorces, no infidelities. So I didn't really have a role model to follow in raising my children alone. I knew they needed a father and I needed a husband, but husbands capable and mature enough to step into a fairly large ready-made family weren't beating down my door. So I wrote a poem about "My Next Husband," about one who would love me and my children, support us, understand us, comfort us, and do just about everything possible for us. It ended by my saying "yes" to Jesus, for he had to be my next husband if I was going to make it.

Looking back, it sure wasn't easy, but it seems that a pattern set in—a pattern that was definitely led by the Spirit of God and that not only helped me once again to find peace and happiness, but that also provided a sound, stable, Catholic home environment for my children. I call this pattern **SPIRIT**, named for its source: Sacraments, Prayer, Involvement, Realities, Investments, and Trust.

Sacraments. I knew from my Catholic upbringing that the sacraments were supposed to provide us with strength. I believed that, but I also needed it to be true. Therefore, the kids and I attended Mass every Sunday (but not at 9:00 A.M.) and went to confession monthly. I would like to say that everything started working out fine, but it didn't happen that way. My two-year-old would pull his shoes and socks off and pick his toes during the consecration (with nuns sitting behind us), someone would always have to go to the bathroom during the sermon, or hands would be squeezed so tight during the Our Father that a fight would break out. But over the years, it paid off. The habit was formed. We discussed sermons in the car going home, we gained new spiritual insights, and the kids and I both made commitments.

A key factor in making the sacraments a part of our lives was my insisting that, yes, we are going to confession tonight, or no, you can't go to the beach before Mass. It would have been so easy to take the lenient road, but setting firm boundaries gave the kids a sense of security. Now that they are all teenagers, I can leave for the weekend for business trips or pleasure, and know that they are going to Mass while I'm gone. I've checked. That's such a wonderful feeling to know that they are getting strength from the sacraments now, even when I'm not home.

Prayer Has Been the Security of Our Family. From the very beginning of my leading the family alone, I got the kids started on the rosary, prayer books, and quiet times. Prayer has been our conversation with our Father/Husband, our requests for many, many favors, our thanksgiving for so many answered petitions, and at times, the safety of our lives. Every meal begins with a prayer, every ambulance or emergency vehicle we hear warrants a prayer, every late night with a missed curfew was spent in prayer, every broken bone, cut finger, surgery, or stomachache was healed with the help of prayer. Developing these habits when my children were little made it much easier when they were older.

One of my favorite prayer books has a wonderful prayer to St. Joseph for safety from drowning. The Lord answered it for us one summer when my nine-year-old was dragged from a ski boat by a bouncing anchor, pulled to the bottom of the lake by the rope wrapped around his ankle, and all of a sudden released and lifted to the surface. He came up screaming and crying, but he was safe.

Another answered prayer for protection: My sixteen-year-old was mysteriously lifted out of a crashed automobile

---

It would have been so easy to take the lenient road, but setting firm boundaries gave the kids a sense of security. Now that they are all teen-agers, I can leave for the week-end, and know that they are going to Mass while I'm gone.

---

by a stranger who just appeared to help him and who disappeared afterwards. My son was a varsity football player, weighing 218 pounds, trapped in the driver's seat in a car that was laying on its side—the driver's side. Bystanders watched the stranger just reach in and pull out my unconscious and very heavy son. The stranger administered first aid, then slipped away when emergency help arrived. My son suffered no permanent injuries other than some glass particles imbedded in his arm.

Money has come from nowhere, job opportunities have fallen into my lap, and strength has come from unexpected sources. Such occurrences have convinced my kids that prayer works, a conviction that only comes from experience. Kids, especially in single-parent families, need prayer more than they need clothes, cars, or money. I say, put the kingdom first, and all these others will be given to you. That's a promise—God's, not mine.

Involvement Is Key. It shapes a child's commitment to the Catholic faith. Allow your kids to be totally involved in areas where they will need to make decisions that affect their lives. This means serving as altar boys, or attending CCD classes, but it also means learning how to become involved in such matters as social issues. My fifteen-year-old son enjoyed being an altar boy so all the girls could see his stud haircut, but that same boy was arrested for demonstrating against a local abortion clinic. My daughter was totally bored with CCD classes, but picketed at an abortionist's home to display her disapproval of his business. If kids express any interest in a public issue or a church problem, I let them come up with ideas of how to get involved in that issue and support them any way I can. If they would prefer to stay in the background, I encourage them to get involved, even if I have to persuade them to come with me. This involvement, activity, and research into what is really happening help form our children's commitment without our having to force-feed them.

Realities. Allow your child to face realities in life for protection against deception. Let them view abortion films to see the horror of the crime. Point out to them how the New Age movement is spiritually false, how advertisers use sex and deceit to push their products, how TV shows display premarital sex, addiction, divorce, and murder as normal and acceptable living. Let them see films on drugs, alcohol, AIDS, car accidents. Let them go to family and friends' funerals. Show them a film on satanic influence in rock music, heavy metal bands, and everyday radio programs. Believe me, they see worse on TV and in the movies like "Nightmare on Elm Street," and "Friday the 13th." At the same time, it's extremely important to give them tools to fight pressures that they face everyday. Teach them the power of prayer, reading Scripture, the use of sacramentals, the frequent reception of the sacraments—for these are the main tools they have at their disposal so that they can resist today's real evils.

Parents who try to protect their children from realities are doing them an injustice. They are throwing them to the wolves with no warning, no protection, leaving them with a sense that they have no one to turn to when they need help. Many kids think their parents aren't aware of what's going on, but, believe me, the kids know. They see album jackets that say "Eat Me." They hear Madonna saying, "I wear crucifixes because I love to look at naked men." They see intercourse in action at the movies. They know young friends whose parents have dragged them into having abortions. And too often we silently let them try to figure it all out on their own. Don't avoid it. Attack it head-on, and use the power of Christ for defense against evil.

Investments. I believe investment in generous giving such as tithing will call down God's gifts to a family. When I first divorced, I was absolutely broke. I had to sell my wedding diamonds to pay for our first month's apartment rent. I received no child support and had no income. I had read somewhere that no matter what you shove out the front door to give to God, he will shove it tenfold into the back door. I couldn't tithe then because I was broke. But my intention was there.

Shortly after my divorce, I started college and applied for work-study programs and welfare, for I couldn't find a job that would pay me enough to support my family. I still couldn't tithe, but I gave what I could.

I earned a bachelor of science degree in industrial management from Purdue University, and Exxon in Houston recruited me to work in computing. At that point I started tithing. Within eight years, I was making a very good salary, purchased an ample home, had three cars in the family, took a trip to Europe, and started my own marketing business on the side.

How does this relate to raising kids Catholic? Even though the Catholic church doesn't insist on tithing as much as some Protestant churches do, we still believe in its power. The kids learned about the importance of giving to God from their earnings. They saw that when I rationalized and held back money to pay a bill that something always seemed to happen to pull that money from me anyway. A car would break down or a vacuum cleaner would burn up. They also saw that when I did tithe, that somehow, from somewhere, we always got enough money. I learned to stick to my commitment to give generously to God and to involve my children in the reality of financial strains. And they learned, in short order, that God keeps his promises.

Trust. This is the most critical factor for depending on your "Husband/Father" to provide the security, peace, love, and financial stability for a family. It is also the most difficult virtue to practice. No matter how many times God pulled me through a disaster, the very next time, I would worry and fret about something minor.

Most of my worries were financial or safety related. I worried about money all the time. I also worried about the children, since I had to leave them so often to go to work very early in the morning and very late at night. The kids would come into my room, put their arms around me, and tell me not to worry, that God would take care of us. They learned faster than I did. Only when I reached my wits' end, when I finally admitted I could not figure out what to do, did I turn to the Lord for help. Once I did that, help always came, and usually in a way I could not have thought about myself.

For example, once I was two months behind in my house payments because of several breakdowns around the house. I had no idea where I would get $2,000 to catch up, so I finally turned to God and asked him to take care of it. Shortly thereafter, my employer announced a retirement of a stock option program, that netted me $2,008. The children never had any major disasters while practically raising themselves alone. Even though ovens and irons were left on (sometimes all day), doors and windows were left open, water was left running, neighborhood homes were burglarized—my children were always fine. We never had a fire, never were robbed, and never were assaulted. In Houston, that is a miracle.

Every day I would put the kids into the hands of their Father in heaven and of Mary, their mother, because I had no choice, and because I finally learned to trust in God's protection. Knowing that someone very loving and powerful is taking care of them gives my kids a real sense of security.

One final word. When you are single with a huge responsibility, the secure place to go is to your church. However, the church has changed so much since we were kids that it might seem strange or unfamiliar. You may not agree with all the new rules, the aftermath of Vatican II, or the new leniency that was not tolerated a few years ago, but remember that the living Christ—present in the tabernacle—is the same Jesus of two thousand years ago and of twenty years ago. The Blessed Sacrament is the most wonderful gift we have. It is Christ, it is Love, it is real. Take advantage of this gift, and teach your children about this miracle that so many of us have taken for granted. Bring your children to say "hello" to Jesus often. Make it a family habit. This Jesus is more than a father, more than a husband, more than a friend, more than a lover. His power is incomprehensible. Reach out to him and embrace him, and your children will become or remain strong, committed Catholics, understanding the gift that they have received.

And don't worry if your child doesn't embrace the faith when you want him or her to do it. Show that child all the love you can, even when he or she is very unlovable. Your persistent love will bring that child to God in ways you cannot imagine. ∎

What Are We Raising Children for, Anyway?

Valuing God's kingdom before all other things has to be an absolute priority in our lives and in the lives of our children.

Ralph Martin

What kind of ambitions and hopes do you have for your children? What do you consider to be the most important values for their lives?

Parenthood begins with these questions. All the techniques of child rearing, all our family activities, all the decisions we make about our children's education, all the advice we give and directions we set, are not nearly as important as our answer to a simple question: What are we raising children for, anyway?

Many parents answer something like this:

"I want my child to have the good things in life that I never had. What I really want for my child is his happiness. I want him to be popular and to succeed at whatever he does."

There are Christian variations on this theme. "I want my child to have a good character," Christians say, and, "I really want my child to marry a Christian."

None of these desires is bad, yet often they reflect a lukewarm rather than a gospel vision for our children's lives. It's not that God doesn't want good things for our children; he has more good in mind for them than we could ever ask for or imagine. God, however, has their eternal happiness in view, and he warns us that the happiness that the world offers is often opposed to his plan.

We find one expression of this in the beatitudes, which say in part: "Blessed are you who are now weeping for you will laugh. Blessed are you when people hate you, when they exclude you and insult you and denounce your name as evil on account of the Son of Man. Rejoice and leap for joy on that day! Behold, your reward will be great in heaven." (Lk 6:21-23).

Jesus doesn't say that any of us will lead trouble-free lives. The blessed—or "the happy" as it is sometimes translated— are those who endure suffering, hardship, shame, and persecution for his sake. He doesn't say that the socially adjusted or physically strong or stylishly dressed or highly intelligent child will automatically be happy. Jesus' followers *will* be happy—they will "rejoice and leap for joy on that day"—but not because of their wealth, intelligence, popularity, or the other things that we most often associate with happiness.

Seek First His Kingdom. We need to keep the primary goal in view. Of course, we want our children to have good things, but if we emphasize them too much, these things will affect their ability to know Jesus Christ. We need to ask ourselves: Will that goal by itself increase our children's desire to follow Jesus?

Good character is important. But what do we mean by "good character"? Is it one that is formed in the Christian virtues of meekness, love, and patience or do we mean only those character traits like friendliness, responsibility, aggressiveness—those that will make our children successful in this life?

Popularity is good. We all want to be liked and respected. But if popularity is an end in itself, will our children compromise their faith in order to be liked by others?

As parents, we are responsible for raising our children to know, love, and serve the Lord. We need to make sure our ambitions for our children reflect the vision of the gospel. We should zealously seek God's will for our children if we don't want to hear the Lord say to us or to them, "Because you are lukewarm, neither hot nor cold, I will spit you out of my mouth" (Rv 3:16).

Valuing God's kingdom before all other things has to be an absolute priority in our lives and the lives of our children. This needs to be a clearly stated goal that guides us in our decisions for our families, and we need to communicate this radical priority in all of our decisions.

Parents should continually ask: Is this activity, friendship, or involvement affecting my child's ability to deny himself and follow Christ? Is this supporting his Christian life or detracting from it? These need to be the standards by which we evaluate decisions for our children.

Not an Option. We are not to present the gospel as an option for our children. We need to train them that it is the obligation of every creature to worship the Creator and to come to know God. Our children may not "naturally" desire to know, love, and serve God. We need to train them in this, just as we train them to brush their teeth and avoid danger on the street. We must train our children to avoid spiritual danger and to seek spiritual guidance. Spiritual realities are no less real, no less objective, than the physical realities we train them for all the time.

Parental authority is one of the main ways that the Holy Spirit works in our children's lives. Children need parents to train them because they don't have the maturity or discernment to decide important matters for themselves wisely. God brings children into the life of the kingdom by giving them mothers and fathers. His grace works through the parents' authority and the children's obedience.

Thus, parents have the responsibility to get their children to live the truth before they fully understand it. As they mature, they'll begin to experience its freeing power.

Many parents today tend to relate to their children as peers, especially when they are cute or intelligent or talented. Children in this situation quickly learn how to lead the family. They control the family by their moods, withdrawing affection, manipulation, and temper tantrums.

Parents must resist such emotional pressure. We can be tempted to win our children's approval by avoiding unpopular decisions. Sometimes we place too much emphasis on having a good relationship with our children. Sometimes we place too much emphasis on how our children feel.

God's grace works through the parents' authority and the children's obedience.

Pressure from our children usually intensifies as they grow older. "You don't trust me!" or "I am old enough to be trusted," they say when parents restrict their activities. Trust has to be earned. Children earn it as they demonstrate their ability to deal maturely with difficult situations. Even so, mature Christians don't expose themselves casually to situations marked by sin.

In fact, teenagers want freedom and independence just when they most need our training and supervision. Children say, "I don't need you. I want to make my own decisions," just when the power of the world, the flesh, and the devil becomes strongest.

Our children's desires to be independent aren't the considerations that matter. We need to be willing to take short-term pain in our relationships with our children for the sake of long-term gain. We must be willing to endure our children's disapproval and their manipulative emotional behavior as they try to make us change our minds.

I asked a young friend of mine what he would have done in his father's place that would have made a difference in his life. He said that he would not have allowed himself to have the companions he had. His parents thought his friends were bad influences, but they let the relationships continue. My friend thought his life would have gone better if his parents had been stricter in setting limits on whom they allowed him to associate with.

The Heart of Christianity Is Obedience in Response to God's Love. Through one man's disobedience, death came into the world. Through one man's obedience, salvation came to the world. All who follow Jesus Christ's example of love must partake in his obedience. Training our children for obedience is essential.

We are not raising our children to be independent individuals who are no longer under any authority when they "grow up."

No one is supposed to be outside of authority. As we mature in the Lord, we are to show greater and greater obedience, not less. Our children will always be under God's authority. We should teach them that they are not going to be free from the obligation of obedience when they reach eighteen or twenty-one years of age.

The freedom we are raising them for is gospel freedom— freedom from the flesh and its selfish desires, freedom from the devil, freedom from worldly values that distort and twist God's plan. Our freedom comes from daily taking up our crosses and following Christ, from living in his presence and the power of the Holy Spirit, and from obeying the Lord.

This is the normal Christian life. It should be our goal for our children—a life worthy of Christ's calling so that they might spend eternity with him in his kingdom. ∎

Think, Pray, & Act

STRENGTHENING YOUR CATHOLIC FAITH

FOR REFLECTION AND DISCUSSION

1. Why is a parent's own faith and behavior important in raising Catholic children? (See articles by Dodds and Nash.)
2. What special concerns must a single parent face? (See article by Cummings.)
3. What scriptural test should I use to set priorities for me and for my family? (See article by Martin.)

TAKING STOCK

Reminder: To make the best use of this feature, write in a notebook, so you can look back and evaluate how you are doing.

1. Am I the kind of Catholic I want my children to become?
2. Do my faith and my behavior show my children how to live as Catholic Christians? If asked, would my children say I did what I told them to do?
3. What goals do I have for my children?
4. Is loving God and putting God first in life a top priority? Have I made it a top priority for my children?

PLAN FOR ACTION

You might want to keep a planning notebook so you can hold yourself accountable for your decisions.

1. Assess the condition of your own faith and relationship with God. You may find the following exercise helpful:
   a. Write a brief paragraph that states as best you can the condition of your relationship with God.
   b. How well do you think you understand what it means to be a Catholic Christian? Make a short list of things you wish you knew better.
   c. Which of the following are a regular part of your life?
      —worship at Sunday Mass
      —daily prayer (rosary, conversational prayer, meditation, quiet reflection, other)
      —the sacrament of reconciliation (going to confession)
      —personal or group Bible study
      —involvement in parish or some Christian service
2. Make a list of changes, additions, or corrections that you would like to make to strengthen your own Christian life.
   a. Arrange your list in priority order, placing the most important at the top.
   b. Consider what it would take to accomplish the most important item.
   c. Make a decision to take the steps necessary to accomplish the item you identify as the top priority.
   d. If you need help to carry through with your decision, get it through your parish or from a Catholic friend. Most of all, ask God to help you to change the things he wants you to change. Ask him to give you the power to be different through the grace of his Holy Spirit.

RESOURCES

Catholic Faith

- Alan Shreck, *Catholic and Christian* (Servant). This is an excellent introduction to what it means to be a Catholic.
- "The Choices We Face." Watch your cable networks for Ralph Martin's inspiring and challenging television series, "The Choices We Face." For information about its availability in your area, write to: The Choices We Face, Servant Ministries, P.O. Box 8617, Ann Arbor, MI, 48107.
- Michael Francis Pennock, *This Is Our Faith: A Catholic Catechism for Adults* (Ave Maria Press).
- John A. Hardon, S.J., *Pocket Catholic Catechism* (Doubleday, Image).

Spiritual Growth

- Bert Ghezzi, *Becoming More Like Jesus: Growth in the Spirit* (Our Sunday Visitor).
- Thomas Green, S.J., *Opening to God: A Personal Guide to Prayer for Today* (Ave Maria Press).
- Henry Libersat, *Way, Truth & Life: Living with Jesus as Personal Savior* (St. Paul Books).
- Carmen Rojas, editor, *Light for Each Day: Growing Closer to God Through Daily Scriptural Prayer and Meditation* (Servant).

Marriage and Family Life

- Pope John Paul II, *On the Family (Familiaris Consortio)* (United States Catholic Conference).
- Randall & Therese Cirner, *10 Weeks to a Better Marriage* (Servant).
- Mitch & Kathy Finley, *Christian Families in the Real World* (Thomas More Press).
- Ralph Martin, *Husbands, Wives, Parents, Children* (Servant).

FOUR

Making Your Home Catholic

If we are going to have Catholic families in Catholic homes, we must work at it. But every little step we take is an invitation to God to be present to us and our children. And he always comes.

Your Family Is a *Holy* Family

Ordinary everyday events, as well as special occasions, are chances to bring our families into God's presence.

Mitch and Kathy Finley

Many families have grown comfortable with living a split-level existence. We tend to view our faith as on one level, and our family relationships as on another. In taking this approach, we are products of the modern age. The ancient Israelites lived in a mental and spiritual world which made no distinctions between the ordinary and the holy. What we call the secular was holy because Yahweh was its Creator, and human life was sacred insofar as it was consistent with this faith.

We can, however, recover a greater sense of the holiness of ordinary things, and of the unity of sacred and secular. We can choose to recognize the deeper dimensions in even the most mundane aspects of family life. We can resolve to overcome the ways in which we tend to separate body and spirit, holy and profane.

Look at the life of any typical family. Most of the significant human events occur there. Birth and death, marriage and childhood, sickness and unemployment—these are but a few of the ordinary events of life, and all belong to a family spirituality. Each event presents an opportunity to recognize and celebrate the presence of God at the heart of family life.

Like many of today's Catholic parents, we grew up with a 1950s-style spirituality which offered a wealth of religious signs, symbols, and rituals. The family rosary in the evening, a special morning prayer to our guardian angel, meatless Fridays, fasting from midnight on, prior to receiving communion the next morning—all these and many more traditions and practices provided a potentially lively network of experiences to nourish the faith of both children and adults.

Today, however, many of the family religious traditions that we grew up with don't seem to "fit" our spiritual needs. To attempt to duplicate for our youngsters the world in which we grew up is futile. The experiences of the holy that we seek are the same, but the forms needed for these experiences to be authentic (not just experiences of religious nostalgia) are sometimes different.

The ritual forms and symbols used in our homes when we were children had a tendency to reflect a piety that was "churchy." Statues, holy water fonts, rote prayer forms—the intention behind these often seemed to be to duplicate as closely as possible moments previously experienced "in church." The ideal seemed to be to make some "churchy" things happen in the home.

However, family relationships and family events are holy in themselves. There is no need for families to behave as if they are in church for their spiritual life to be all that it can be. We need to recognize and celebrate Christ present in the dynamics of the ordinary—then gradually, patiently, develop appropriate ways to nourish our intimacy with this presence. Many Catholic families today try to found their shared faith on the conviction that all of ordinary life is one and is holy.

Daily Events. Opportunities for a family to celebrate the sacred in their life together fall into two general categories— "daily" and "special." The key daily event in almost every family's experience is the evening meal. It is here that, potentially, a family is most fully family. (Close your eyes for a moment and try to visualize the family in which you grew up. . . . Most people report that they automatically picture their family around the dinner table.)

When a family gathers at table for an ordinary meal, far more than stomachs are filled. We bring more than physical hunger to our gathering. To share a meal is to make visible and build up the love which is at the heart of family life.

The family meal is an ordinary/sacred opportunity to know one another in the breaking of the bread—to know intimacy with the Lord through intimacy with one another. In the sharing of ordinary food and conversation the sacred is likely to emerge, from one day to the next.

From an authentic Catholic perspective, the family meal is naturally eucharistic. To share a meal is to say that we care for one another. We give thanks for the ways in which we love and serve one another, for the ways that we are gifts to one another. Thus we nourish the personal and faith relationships that bind us together.

We need to be realistic, of course. Mealtimes can be as filled with conflict as any other aspect of family life. But the point is that in the family meal there is at least a chance to listen to one another, an opportunity for some prayer, a bit of song, a moment of quiet, a candle's flame, and a brief ritual to mark our gathering. The family meal has a potential for simple but satisfying family religious rituals. This is one reason we personally go into near apoplexy at the very suggestion that a family gather around a television set, food-laden plates on their laps.

Other ordinary daily events which have a deep natural holiness waiting to be unlocked are: coming home and leaving home, hugs, and taking time to reflect on the day that is just beginning or just drawing to a close. Times of forgiveness and reconciliation are fertile ground for recognizing the presence of the Healer. Small, sometimes momentary ways to evoke the sacred in these and many other ordinary family events can be created by a family that tries to be sensitive to the inherent holiness of their life together.

Making Sunday Special

Begin the new week with the celebration of the Eucharist. Go together as a family if at all possible. Play special "Sunday music" on the stereo as everyone gets ready for church. Wear your "Sunday best." Don't read the Sunday papers before Mass as it may distract you from what you are about. At your Sunday breakfast or brunch, choose a special meal prayer that you don't use on other days of the week. The Jewish people pray: "Light and rejoicing to Israel: Sabbath, soother of sorrows, comfort of downtrodden Israel, healing the hearts that were broken. Banish despair: here is hope come!"

Resolve not to do any unnecessary work. What does need doing (making the beds, setting the table, doing the dishes) can be done by the whole family together.

Special Events in family life are also sometimes neglected as potential doors to the sacred. It is taken for granted that a physical birth will lead to the spiritual rebirth of baptism; that a marriage will begin with a wedding liturgy in church; that a death in the family will mean a church funeral; and that a seriously ill family member will receive a sacramental anointing at the hands of a priest.

But what about the family context where the events that are marked in "official" ways have their roots? If each of these events is holy, it is holy first of all because it is holy in and of itself, though sometimes in hidden ways. At such times in-the-home family rituals are appropriate—even necessary—to the health of the family spirit.

Perhaps the special family event that is most "ordinary" is the celebration of a birthday. This is an event loaded with religious significance, if only it is recognized. The family celebrates the gift that the birthday person is to the family as

continued on next page

Play the piano, read a book, go swimming, play ball. Go to a museum, visit the park, the beach, the zoo, or the mountains. Family members can take turns planning the Sunday outing.

If there is a special ballgame or television program that is truly worth watching, invite the family to participate in it. If some family members are not interested, they should feel encouraged to pursue an interest of their own. Choose a family video to watch on the VCR together if you have one.

Whatever you undertake on Sunday, do it in a spirit of mutual understanding and care for one another. Try to do everything without haste or anxiety. Sunday is a day to be fully human and to taste of heaven.

Gertrud M. Nelson

a whole. In addition to the "secular" rituals of singing "Happy Birthday" and blowing out candles on a cake, special prayers can be included. A song may be added which expresses the family's gratitude for this person. The family says, in effect, "We are happy that God gave you to us. We wouldn't be us without you!"

The ordinary lives of ordinary families are filled with the extraordinary—the sacred is just around every corner. It is in family intimacy, first of all in our families and in our friendships, that God is present and active. Woven in and out of the ordinary lives we share are the countless, vine-like roots of the divine mystery. ∎

Family Prayer— Getting Started

Suggestions for parents who sense a lack in their present family prayer and want to instill a sense of Christian celebration in their home.

Dolores Curran

Whenever I speak to parents on the development and enjoyment of prayer and celebration in the home, I find I don't need to sell them on the idea as much as on confidence and method.

One mother articulated it this way, "I know it seems ridiculous but our family is embarrassed to pray aloud and sing together."

Ridiculous? Not at all. It's a very natural reaction, particularly in a church where private devotion has been the rule. A family simply doesn't leap from silent grace and rote evening prayers to a vibrant, guitar-thumping, soul-baring celebration. Like the church, the family glides into a post-Vatican II attitude toward prayer.

Even the terminology is different today. What we called *devotions* as children, we now call *celebrations*.

The family devotions which marked our childhood consisted mainly of the rosary, an occasional novena, and shrine or saint prayers. Most of them were printed in leaflets. There was very little spontaneous prayer. Individual comment on the Gospels was unheard of, and most family devotions were scheduled by the calendar: May, October, and Lent being the chief periods.

Since the term *devotions* carries the connotation of private prayer, we needed to coin a new phrase for praying together. Hence, the word *celebration* which includes both prayer together and enjoyment, the two elements parents find so difficult to blend. Why?

Because we don't see prayer as something to enjoy together. Prayers were something we learned. Our parents taught us prayers because they were taught that was their responsibility. (More than one parent breathed a sigh of sanctified relief when the five-year-old finally managed the Apostles' Creed.)

Obviously many parents have been able to find ways to teach their children to pray together. Witness the number of ten-to-fifteen-year-olds who uninhibitedly enjoy the Mass and other liturgies together. Many parents who have overcome uncomfortable and embarrassing hurdles to family prayer and celebrations have some suggestions to offer the rest of us. More encouragingly, they tell us that the transition is worth it, that once the awkwardness is faced and overcome, the family really can enjoy prayers and celebrations together—as unbelievable as it may seem to us.

For parents who sense a lack in their present family prayers and want to instill a sense of Christian celebration in their home, here are some thoughts and suggestions.

Why Pray at All? I'm afraid this one has to be hit head-on. Why do we want our children to pray? To set a good habit of praying? To have someone to turn to when the need arises? To carry out an obligation? To seek favors? Why?

Parents have different reasons for wanting their children to pray consistently. Since the reason largely determines the method, parents have to look at the reason honestly. And it's high time we did.

My husband, Jim, and I want to make God a real person to our children, someone with whom they can converse casually and enjoyably. We feel memorization thwarts openness. It can be a form of escape from real contact with God. Naturally, other parents may take a somewhat different tack.

Many parents today aren't really sure why they teach their children prayer. "Because we're supposed to . . ." is a pretty lame excuse today. A child's absorption of prayer is no indication of his faith. Once parents sit down and discuss together why they see a value in teaching their children to pray, their job will become easier.

Talking with God—How Do We Go about It? Since our whole orientation toward prayers is a mixture of awe, fear, reverence, obligation, supplication, thanksgiving, and penitence, it's very hard for us to talk to God for no reason. We tend to set aside a particular time to do it—before meals, at bedtime, and on Sunday mornings. If something urgent comes up, like a possible disease or promotion, we find ourselves talking with God more frequently. Otherwise our prayer pattern is a scheduled one.

Therefore, it makes us quite uncomfortable to think of a casual and constant conversation with God. An older friend of mine saw the play, *Fiddler on the Roof,* in which the milkman chats with God in a delightfully casual and sometimes irreverent way. Afterwards she said, "I really liked the play, but it made me nervous for some reason. Like he was just a little sacrilegious, you know."

Her nervousness sprang from a lifetime of keeping a respectful chasm between God and herself. Sometimes I think we would have been much better off being just a little "sacrilegious" at times. But the grown-up Christian knows that if he is to become warm and open to God, he has to overcome some childhood hangups. What many of us parents don't realize is that the hangups and awkwardness are more on our part than our children's. They find casual prayer and family celebrations quite enjoyable.

We have a lot of great men and women in our heritage whose God was very real and very involved in their daily lives. A good way to start a more open response toward God in children is by making them familiar with some of the Old Testament characters who spoke to God comfortably—and daily. You can start by retelling the story of Jonah. You can bring Jonah to life by translating his words into kids' language. For example tell them how Jonah argued with God. Jonah said, "Look, God . . . Nineveh is far away and right now it's too hot for long trips."

The Old Testament is filled with stories of people who talked with God. The New Testament is filled with stories of people who talked with Jesus. Let's start teaching openness to God by making our children familiar with the Bible, something we were not familiar with as children.

Bible stories won't do it alone, however. If we don't want to teach our children embarrassment and discomfort toward open prayer, we're going to have to start overcoming our own. This means making confident oral responses at Mass, not mumbled "I-feel-foolish" kinds of noises. It means saying some meaningful graces, not formulas. It means being able to talk *about* God without feeling foolish. We must become more open ourselves, free to say to a child leaving for school, "God keep you today." Free to say, "Well, I talked it over with God . . . ."

Family Prayer and Celebration—How Do We Start It?

Families differ. So will their celebrations. My suggestions

here are merely guidelines for the great number of people who ask, "But can you give us some hints on getting into a family pattern of prayer?" Above all, no parent should feel guilty if he or she doesn't choose to inaugurate an Advent wreath ceremony or nameday festivity. The celebrations I mention are just examples to be used if the family feels drawn to them.

Most parents with whom I talk are gravely concerned over the state of their children's daily prayers. Most say their children don't say any morning prayers and their evening prayers are rote and reluctant. "How can we teach them to pray and like it?" they ask.

The age of the children will largely determine the approach to family prayer. Children under nine are still enthusiastic over anything new and will cooperate if the family starts a prayer custom in the evening. Those over nine have pretty well adopted their parents' awkwardness toward open prayer. Still, many families tell me that if there are younger children, the older one can be drawn into the family attempt simply by watching their little brothers and sisters.

Our own evening prayer is quite unspectacular. For several years now we have been meeting before bedtime for a ten-minute prayer celebration around the dining room table. One of the kids lights a candle (after squabbling over whose turn it is), and each of us says a short spontaneous prayer. There is Jim's prayer for the whole family, and then we sing a rousing hymn.

But are we flexible! Sometimes, instead of praying, we ask Beth to read a Bible story or ask Mike to explain his catechism work. Sometimes we talk about a newsworthy event and how it ties in with God and us. We did that when there was an impending flood. "Why should we ask God to stop it when he's sending it?" asked Mike. We spent our evening prayer time discussing that on a preschool theology level. Sometimes, we sing "America the Beautiful" for our hymn. During Lent, we use a booklet for family devotions.

Because this time of day frequently finds me at my lowest level of patience, the atmosphere is sometimes too charged for praying. We all know it would be hypocritical to put on our "church faces" and pray after a scene about homework or dirty clothes. So we play it by ear. On such nights, we frequently substitute individual prayers.

We make a lot of mistakes. All of our celebrations aren't successes. When we feel we are getting bored with the sameness of evening prayer, we stop for a month and read from a children's Bible instead. As the children get older, we hope to use other books with them, children's books with a message relevant to Christianity, and certainly some biographies of people who lived for others.

Families with teenagers may find the period immediately following dinner the best time. Frequently, such a family finds it hard to get together any time of the day other than dinner. Kids this age are too hungry for a "long grace" or Bible reading before dinner and have too many activities to rely upon a bedtime prayer hour.

Advent wreath customs are becoming more popular, if for no other reason than offsetting the materialistic attitude surrounding Christmas. Many families use this custom to sneak into an ongoing family prayer in the evening. Most parishes have Advent wreath leaflets if the parents want to inaugurate this beautiful tradition in their home.

Summing up, let's stop fretting over when and where and how to teach youngsters their prayers. Instead, let's teach them that everything in life can be prayer. We were told that but were taught prayers. This time let's teach it and show our children we believe it. ■

Making Big Christians Out of Little Ones

*It's never too late to start, but
don't wait another day.*

Mary Ann Kuharski

Speaking as a mom in the trenches, the best advice I could give a young couple eager to make big Christians out of little ones is:

1. Start While You and Your Children Are Young. If your kids aren't used to going to church with you, praying *together* in the home, or observing religious practices, it's never too late to begin. But don't wait another day.

Changing old ways or bad habits becomes all the more difficult with each passing year, especially if children are entering their teens. These are the years that nature and their peers urge them to question many facets of their lives. You can bet they're going to rebel if a parent suddenly suggests saying the daily rosary during Lent, discussing a Scripture passage, or attending Mass together, if such practices are not ones that youngsters have grown up with.

2. Attend Mass Together as a Family. Unless sickness, a new baby, or conflicting schedule prevents otherwise, this is an occasion for the entire family. No matter how distracting, a special unifying bond is created by sitting as a family in the same pew week after week and publicly worshiping God. It helps, by the way, to sit toward the front where little ones are close to the action and can see the priest and what's going on.

For those who have rambunctious preschoolers, don't give up. Take them to the back of the church if you must. Remember, with time a youngster will begin to imitate the reverence and silence they see in the people around them.

3. Make the Lord's Day Special. With pressures coming at families six days a week, Sunday should be the one day we put away our office work, home "fix-it" chores, and unpleasant tasks, and plan something fun and relaxing for the whole family. Doing this is one positive way of letting our children know that Sundays are special to us because of our love for God.

continued on next page

The Family That Eats Together ...
Dinner Table Guidelines

Family experts suggest these rules to make the dinner hour a positive experience.

1. Give the dinner hour priority. Expect this of all family members.
2. Agree upon tasks of preparation, serving, clearing, and cleanup. Family members are not guests. They are part of a team and responsible to it.
3. Give every person at the table a chance to talk about the people and events in his or her day.
4. Listen with your eyes as well as your ears. Look at the person talking. Avoid interrupting or making putdowns.
5. Have special family holidays and awards dinners occasionally. This sustains the notion that eating and being together as a family is one of the best times of the day.
6. Don't use the dinner table as an arena to work out family

continued on next page

4. Pray Together as a Family. Praying together before meals is a must. In fact, when our youngsters are old enough, we often let them choose an additional reading, besides the "Bless Us O Lord." It makes the child feel a special part and demonstrates the importance we place on thanking God for our food.

Hint: Be sure to help your child select the reading. One evening at mealtime our daughter, Chrissy, asked if she could read a new prayer from her religion book. As a first grader, she read well but very S L O W L Y. We naively consented and then sat for nearly ten minutes with our gravy and potatoes turning cold and dry, as she trudged

fights or to discipline. If you do, it will overshadow the joy of being together.

7. Don't make a big issue over manners either by frequency of reprimand or harshness of tone—just offer friendly reminders as needed.

8. Don't force children to eat more than they want. If you force them to unhook their natural appetite mechanisms, this could lead to an eventual overeating problem. On the other hand, it is OK to encourage them to try one bite of everything.

9. Don't use food as a reward or punishment.

10. Don't avoid talking about your day at work even if there were problems. Otherwise, kids will grow up with a ridiculously rosy picture or feel you've shut them out.

Barbara Burthoff

through the Apostles' Creed. After that, we made up a selection sheet of short dinnertime prayers.

Sunday should be the one day we put away our work, chores, and unpleasant tasks, and plan something fun and relaxing for the whole family.

---

5. *Invest Effort in Evening Prayers.* Here is where it's important to start young. And don't ask too much of your children.

As young parents we started with the "Angel of God." When we wanted to introduce the rosary we knew there would be resistance. The younger children were too small to sit still and the older ones were used to shorter prayers. We started with one decade. Gradually we increased it to two decades, then three and eventually the entire rosary. Today our little ones proudly take turns leading a decade.

In our family, we found that even when it's been one of those hope-tomorrow-is-better days, there is a calming, soothing, and tenderly close experience that comes from kneeling together for nightly prayers. "The rosary takes twelve minutes and is the most powerful weapon outside of the Mass we have," my husband often reminds the kids.

6. *Make Use of Sacramentals.* The use of holy water, blessed candles, palms, and other sacramentals can add meaning to children's faith and understanding. Michael, our enthusiastic four-year-old, imitated our every action at church. When we stood, he stood, when we genuflected, so did he.

When we blessed ourselves with holy water as we entered church, he too dipped his hand in the font. The imitation ended, however, when we saw him immediately put his fingers into his mouth—sucking off the dripping water. To Michael this ritual with water only made sense when done for the purpose of quenching thirst. Once we brought home our own bottle of holy water, hung up a font, and began the practice of blessing our children and each other, Michael not only learned to bless himself properly, but he now understands its meaning and use.

The use of holy water, blessed candles, palms, and other sacramentals can add meaning to children's faith and understanding.

Lighting a vigil candle at church and offering a special prayer for someone you know is another good way of making your faith visible and obvious to your children. By your actions you are saying, "I believe prayer helps and I know God hears."

7. *Create Catholic Customs and Celebrations.* We want our kids to know that we believe our faith is something to rejoice over and celebrate. As such, we make a big deal every time a family member is baptized, confirmed, or receives First Holy Communion. We call them our "sacrament parties" and we hope our children will long remember the special foods, baked goods, and relatives and friends that made up our sacramental celebrations.

Create your own family traditions with special emphasis on the holidays and sacred seasons. One of our favorite Advent wreaths was made by our little ones, using four candles and an egg carton with imitation grass around the edges. This is a simple, yet beautiful custom that has drawn our family together in prayer.

Becoming an Advent Angel, patterned on the popular Kris Kringle custom, is an annual practice our children—including the teens and young adults—really look forward to. Each person draws the name of another family member and secretly prays for them during Advent. In addition, the Angel sends notes with little surprises or does a household chore for his or her person.

Lent is another "faith-builder" if used by parents to promote the value of "giving and giving up" for the love of God. We talk to our kids about what things we're giving up and let them know how difficult it is for us. We've found that they in turn don't want to be outdone in commitment and endurance, and eagerly rise to the challenge of penitential sacrifice.

8. Presenting the Image of God. We must never forget that in our children's eyes we can do no wrong. We are like God to them. That should be reason enough to send every parent trembling in prayer to the Lord asking for direction and grace in order to be the kind of example and guiding force needed to make big Christians out of little ones. ◼

Think, Pray, & Act

STARTING FAMILY PRAYER

FOR REFLECTION AND DISCUSSION

1. Why can ordinary family life be said to be "holy"? (See article by the Finleys.)
2. What steps help prepare a family for praying openly together? (See article by Curran.)
3. How can a family get started praying together? (See articles by Curran and Kuharski.)
4. What are some practices that can help create a Catholic home? (See article by Kuharski.)

TAKING STOCK

One More Reminder: If you decide to make use of the following sections at the end of each chapter, it would be a good idea to write your response in a notebook. In later chapters, you will want to look back and see how you are doing.

1. Take an inventory of Catholic practices in your family. If you like, use the following list.
    —family prayer (at meals, before bedtime, other)
    —read Scripture or Catholic books to the family
    —have special meal on Sunday (brunch or dinner)
    —make Sunday special by doing something as a family
    —worship together at Mass on Sunday
    —subscribe to Catholic magazines and have Catholic books
    —celebrate seasons and Christian holidays

—celebrate in special way birthdays, baptisms, First Communion, confirmation, and so on
—make use of parish programs such as religious education
—decorate with Catholic Christian art
—teach the children Catholic prayers, such as the rosary, and use these to pray as a family
—other (specify)

2. If you have introduced some of these practices, which seem to be working well? Which don't seem to work?

PLAN FOR ACTION

Remember to write your plans down, perhaps keeping them in a notebook so you can easily check on your progress.

1. If you have not introduced your family to praying together, start the practice as soon as possible. The following suggestions will help you:
   a. Review the advice in the articles by Curran and Kuharski, jotting down points that relate to your family circumstances.
   b. Couples should agree on an approach before presenting the matter to the family. A single parent might want to solicit the advice of a trustworthy friend and fellow parent before deciding on an approach and presenting the matter to the family.
   c. Teach the family in advance why and how you are going to pray.
   d. Start with a modest effort that you can sustain for a long time.
   e. Be patient, and once you start, stick to your guns.
   f. Start today.

2. If you are already having family prayer, you should consider introducing another family practice.

ACTIVITY

Introduce your family to praying aloud together. As a way of helping family members learn that God is a person they can talk to, teach them to pray aloud together. The following tips will help you:

- Choose a day and time when all will be present.
- If it's at a mealtime, be sure food preparation will not interfere with the prayer time.
- Tell the family your plan ahead of time. Ask everyone to think of something they can thank God for and something they can ask him to do.
- You might begin with a short reading from Scripture, such as the Gospel of Luke, chapter 11, verses 5 to 13 (the story of the friend who comes at midnight, asking for bread).
- Instruct the family that you are going to go twice around the table person by person. The first time each one will thank God out loud for something. The second time each one will ask God for something for him or herself or for another family member.
- Teach everyone to address God directly. They should say, "Father, I thank you for ...," "God, please help me with ...," or "Jesus, ..." rather than the impersonal and indirect, "I want to thank God for ...."
- Mom or Dad should start, setting an example that can be imitated.
- Give special help in advance to very little ones or older kids who you might expect will have a hard time with the experience.
- Consider making this type of prayer a regular part of your family life.

RESOURCES

Bibles

(See **Resources** for chapter one as well.)

- *The Daily New Testament with Psalms & Proverbs* (Servant Publications).
- *The Catholic One Year Bible* (Our Sunday Visitor).

Prayer Books

- *The Catholic Prayer Book,* compiled by Michael Buckley (Servant Publications).
- *My First Prayer Book* (Regina Press).
- M. Basil Pennington, O.C.S.O., *Prayer times: Morning, Midday, Evening* (Doubleday Image).
- Mickey and Terri Quinn, *How to Pray with Your Children* (Liturgical Press).
- David E. Rosage, *Praying the Scriptural Rosary* (Servant).
- Louis M. Savary, *The Catholic Children's Prayer Book* (Regina Press).
- Bernadette McCarver Snyder, *Everyday Prayers for Everyday People* (Our Sunday Visitor).

Magazines and Periodicals

Having Catholic magazines available helps make a home Catholic. You might want to examine some of the following periodicals to see if you like them. Try borrowing some issues from your parish library or from Catholic friends or neighbors. Some magazines will send you one free copy and an invoice, which you can cancel if you are not satisfied. I suggest you consider this representative list:

- **Catholic Digest** publishes each month material of interest to Catholics gathered mainly but not exclusively from the Catholic press (P.O. Box 64090, St. Paul, MN 55164).

- **The Catholic Answer** is a question-and-answer magazine that explains the Catholic faith in clear, concise terms (200 Noll Plaza, Huntington, IN 46750).
- **Catholic World** is a bimonthly magazine that devotes each issue to a topic of importance to Catholics. Published by Paulist Press, (997 Macarthur Blvd., Mahwah, NJ 07430).
- **The Family** is a monthly that "stresses the special place of the family within society as an irreplaceable center of life, love, and faith." Published by the Daughters of St. Paul (50 St. Paul's Avenue, Boston, MA 02130).
- **God's Word Today** is a monthly magazine edited by George A. Martin. It provides a daily reading program that goes through the Bible book by book, and an issue on biblical themes is published about three times a year (P.O. Box 7705, Ann Arbor, MI 48107).
- **Liguorian** is a popularly written general interest Catholic magazine published monthly by the Redemptorists (One Liguori Drive, Liguori, MO 63057-9999).
- **New Covenant** is a monthly that focuses on renewal in the Catholic church, especially in its charismatic, ecumenical, family, evangelistic, and community dimensions. Published by Servant Publications (P.O. Box 7009, Ann Arbor, MI 48107).
- **New Heaven/New Earth** is a monthly magazine of teaching, inspiration, and commentary, published by the People of Praise (107 S. Greenlawn, South Bend, IN 46617-3429).
- **Our Sunday Visitor,** "the national Catholic family weekly," offers a variety of news, features, teaching, and commentary (200 Noll Plaza, Huntington, IN 46750).
- **Share the Word** is published by The Paulist National Catholic Evangelization Association (3031 Fourth Street NE, Washington, DC 20017). This bimonthly paperback gives background and commentary on Sunday Scripture readings through the year and recommends daily readings that help one prepare for Sunday readings.

- **U.S. Catholic** is a monthly general interest Catholic magazine published by the Claretians (205 W. Monroe St., Chicago, IL 60606).
- **Veritas** Catholic Youth Magazine, a popularly written bimonthly magazine especially for teenagers and young adults (Veritas Communications, P.O. Box 8033, Syracuse, NY 13217).
- **The Word Among Us** is published by The Mother of God Community of Potomac, Maryland (P.O. Box 3645, Washington, DC 20037). This monthly magazine follows the church year, taking a lectionary reading from each day of the liturgical cycle, interpreting it, and giving a meditation.

FIVE

Shaping Kids Catholic

*Training children in prayer, worship, the sacra-
ments, and Scripture study are the ways and means
of forming them in the Catholic faith.*

Worshiping
Together at Mass

*Attending Mass together may be hectic, but it is the
heart of Catholic family life.*

Richard and Patricia Easton

One of the few constants in our family's often chaotic life
is Sunday Mass attendance. Much planning, labor, and grace
have been essential, however, to make Sunday services
meaningful celebrations for us and our three children. To
arrive at church smiling and on time, we have regularly
acted the roles of efficiency expert, despot, costumer,
plumber, cook, prophet—our list of roles lengthens as our
children mature from infants to teens.

Many Sundays Mom and Dad have arrived red-faced and
tight-lipped at the church door. A few Sundays we have
even departed the church more frenzied than when we
entered. At those moments we wondered why bother shep-

herding this unruly flock into the house of God? In calmer moments, we knew that learning together about Mass participation was necessary for us all to grow in our faith. Even when our children were very young we would no more have withheld Mass from them than denied them food and affection. Family participation in Mass, we decided, was a key to keeping our children Catholic. But in order to be successful at this we had to make Mass for them the nurturing experience it is for us.

Worshiping Together as a Family. The Mass, as an act of communal rather than private worship, has had real significance for us—our dating included Mass attendance, a bit unusual since Pat wasn't Roman Catholic. She loved Mass and our participation. She even began taking instructions before I had given my commitment and the engagement ring. Singing and praying joyfully with family and friends before the altar came easily:

> The cup of blessing that we bless, is it not a participation in the blood of Christ? The bread that we break, is it not a participation in the body of Christ? Because the loaf of bread is one, we, though many, are one body, for we all partake of the one loaf (1 Cor 10:16-17).

The lusty wailing of our firstborn brought special concerns about Mass participation, as it does to most new parents. We decided never to inflict Elizabeth's newborn distress on our worshiping congregation, nor to inflict on her a sense of guilt for disturbances she couldn't help. Supportive parishes provide cry-rooms and sometimes nurseries staffed by volunteers.

If cry-room or nursery service is not available, you should try to set up your own informal nursery care, perhaps in a church building and maybe with the involvement of other new parents. Certainly, volunteers, from doting seniors to responsible teens, can be found to play with babies. Even when a nursery is necessary, the children—though not in the church during Mass—have been part of the family's trip to church.

Our infant from the first weeks of life was a blessedly over-fed, placid creature, who loved to nap in our arms. By a regular schedule of feedings and a morning of intense activity we usually managed to get her to nap for sixty minutes. Within thirteen months we had an infant son in our arms too. The regimen of activity, feeding, and dressing now required both parents, but we stood together with the babies on our shoulders, the post-Mass delight of the congregation.

The Trials and Travails. We found participation at Mass when the children were anywhere from two to five years old not only the most difficult, but also the most valuable formative times. We enjoyed our children's imitative behavior, the two- and three-year-olds standing attentively, faces shining, struggling to mimic responses:

Our Father who art an Evan
Harold be Thy Name.

We also experienced our share of unexpected verbal assaults, pew vaulting, and aisle escapes. (Will we ever recover from Rick's end run to the altar?) On the scene, Mom responded to such outbreaks with loving hugs—a real vision of post-Vatican II unity. Dad had a tendency to hiss threats on life and limb—a real product of strict regimentation. Dad admits that Mom's nurturing produced gurgles of delight rather than disruptive shrieks of protest.

We both knew enough about child psychology to realize that it is often impossible for a two- or three-year-old to sit still for long. This was especially true of our youngest, Matthew, who spent at least half of every Mass in our church's cry-room running his cars across the floor. After Mass, when necessary, we did administer discipline—gentle but firm. "You were disruptive today at Mass. We think you should sit quietly for ten minutes to give to Jesus the time you missed."

The codes of proper behavior were never stressed as much as the joys of attending Mass. We decided early that a child's appreciation of that joy depended on our visibly acting joyful. Smiles had to replace scowls, no matter the emergency in church. Rather than stressing how their behavior "was simply impossible," we stressed what behavior was possible—remembering that they were only children learning how to appreciate the Mass. Also we had to control our own moods to avoid Sunday morning grouchiness. Clothes had to prepared the night before, shoes located, hair done, our baths taken. We had to fit our intentions to our actions.

Who, Me, Go To Confession?

One of our sons accidentally made his first confession when an elderly priest short-circuited our parish's plan to reverse the traditional order and introduce kids first to the Eucharist and then to the sacrament of reconciliation. To prevent this from happening, he ran our son's entire class through the confessional, without advance notice or preparation. Our boy was very shaken by the experience, so Janet comforted him. "Just look at it this way," she said, "it will be a lot easier next time."

"You mean I have to do that *again*?" he replied.

That was twenty years ago, and over the years that son has come to appreciate the sacrament of reconciliation. The attitudes of our other six adult children toward confession vary. Some are more eager than others to avail themselves of this sacrament, but all of them recognize its value and take advantage of it.

We took three foundational stances during our children's

Other Rituals to Make Sunday Special. We have used other family rituals to nurture the central ritual of family worship. We often celebrate Sundays with special family meals— morning and evening. The addition of flowers or china on the table, let alone special fruit or baked goods, mark for our children the day's special importance.

The children's school years have produced new challenges and rewards. Fortunately we have had the support of our priests and parochial school faculty in the children's formal religious education. The children attend weekday Mass once a week with their classmates. Either one or both of us attend as often as possible to show the children that for us Mass is not just for Sundays and because "we have to."

But also with school days we have had to deal with the occasional negative attitudes of peers toward church. Still

continued on next page

---

early years that were instrumental in laying the groundwork for their later appreciation of confession:

- *First,* we insisted that they recognize that "right" and "wrong" were absolutes. We taught them that no matter what new popular theory they could cite to excuse sinful behavior, they could not live life comfortably very long if they were not in the right place spiritually. We immediately confronted every effort at rationalization, pointing out the fallacy in such claims as, "C'mon, Dad! Even Queen Victoria would wink at that."

- *Second,* we clearly laid out a process for "getting right" spiritually. they had committed some offense, there were simple procedures for repairing their wrongdoing. We trained them to repent to people they had hurt— taking responsibility for the offense and asking forgiveness. Conversely, when someone repented and asked them for forgiveness, we expected the children to forgive and put the problem to rest.

continued on next page

struggling to smile cheerfully, we try to remember that rebelling is sometimes part of the process of growing up. We find ourselves still dressing the children, or more often, directing our teenagers to re-dress themselves. "No, I don't think jeans and a tee shirt are appropriate. No, I don't think we want everyone staring at the glitter in your teased hair instead of at the altar." The same rules of clothes preparation that applied in preschool days seem to apply again for teens.

We now find ourselves after church, hissing (but still trying to smile), "You're supposed to kneel up. And please—sing!"

And we hear, "No one else does! Sometimes you two are such old fogeys!"

Of course, these challenges have led to a new type of discipline—at their age, the discipline of conversations. At least, we have been able to discuss with them the Mass as a public, not a private, act of prayer. And we have been able to explain that as a family we believe in attending Mass regularly as a sign of our active relationship with Christ and the church community. Toward this end, we encourage the

Of course, repenting to God involved going to the sacrament of reconciliation.

• *Third*, we always expected our children to *do* what they were taught was right while they were still learning *why* it was right. We are always puzzled by parents who do not insist on obedience because their child "doesn't understand."

In our family we approached physical health and spiritual health in the same way. We never spent an inordinate amount of time explaining to our children why they should go to the doctor or the dentist. And we didn't wait until they understood all of the theological concepts and church children to greet their friends after Mass as we make a point to stop and exchange news with ours.

The Rewards. Our efforts have had their rewards. One of the most recent occurred on the first Sunday after Matthew made his First Communion. Year after year, poor Matt had looked so sad as the rest of us shared in communion. Our hearts pounded with joy to see Matt's serious look of satisfaction and his brother and sister's smiles, as he received the host, surrounded by his family.

On another Sunday, we found that due to a long sermon and communion lines, we had to leave church before the priest did if we were to make it to our new nephew's christening, half-way across the city. We lingered until the final hymn began and then ran for the car. The children were shocked. Nine-year-old Matt sputtered, "I can't believe it! If you went to Grandma's house for dinner, would you jump up as soon as you finished eating and leave?" Red-faced, we laughed, knowing we had shared with him our love of the Mass.

continued on next page

teaching regarding attendance at Mass before we insisted on their going. When one of our children has a headache, we commonly ask, "Have you tried taking an aspirin?" Similarly, if one is a little depressed, we are just as likely to ask, "Have you been to confession lately?"

We believe that what made all this work for us is our attitude as parents toward the spiritual dimension of our family life—our willingness to repent to our children when we were wrong; our eagerness to forgive them for their wrongdoing; and our love and respect for the church and the sacraments, including the sacrament of reconciliation.

Van and Janet Vandagriff

We will, no doubt, have more challenges to meet. What keeps us searching for answers is the desire to keep open the channels of grace that the Mass offers for both ourselves and our children. We are convinced that focusing on family participation in the Mass during these early years is essential to help our children understand and keep their faith. ■

Getting Your Kids into the Bible

*Family Bible study may seem like a nightmare,
but with a little grace you can get through
the obstacles and get started.*

Jim Auer

Don Bradford wakes up in a cold sweat from the same horrible dream for the third night in a row. The scenario is always the same: He walks into the living room where his three children are staring at an early evening game show. He is carrying a Bible.

He waits until an accountant from Long Island wins a new convertible and a year's supply of creme rinse. Then he announces, "Kids, I think we should spend part of our evening reading the Bible."

Three heads turn toward him in unison. For a moment, there is silence. Then his oldest child collapses on the sofa in uncontrolled spasms of laughter. The middle child eloquently rolls eyeballs, while the youngest says, "Aw, Dad, do we hafta?"

Colita Washington is another parent who wakes up from a similar bad dream. In her nightmare she and her daughter are discussing some recent problems at school. "Maybe we should see what the Bible has to say about that," Colita suggests. Her daughter stares at her in transfixed, open-mouthed silence for a moment and then says, "*Mothe-e-er*— are you serious? That stuff is, like, so incredibly old! Are you on a religious kick or something?"

Okay, Don and Colita are fictional and their nightmares are perhaps a little exaggerated—but not much. An anonymous survey would probably unearth thousands of parents who long to entice their children into Scripture but, well, chicken out, especially if their children are above ten or eleven. Dark imaginings of scenes like those above inhibit the attempt.

Ghosts from the past may inhibit the attempt too: "We did that once before, and it was boring." "We tried that a couple years ago, and we could never understand it, remember?" "*You* used to say the Bible was outdated—how come you changed your mind all of a sudden?"

If you're not victimized by any of these inhibitions, wonderful. Bear with me for a few paragraphs. But if you are, you must take these intimidating bulls by their proverbial horns. And speaking of things proverbial, a Chinese proverb applies well here: "The best way out is always through."

First, a brief disclaimer: We are not heading into an article which might feature a tabloid headline like, "Revealed at Last—The Hidden but Simple Secrets of Getting Your Kids into the Bible!" What follows is more like a very general recipe. Vary the ingredients—even add or subtract some— according to taste, or in this case, according to your family's situation.

If your suggestion to get involved with Scripture doesn't receive the same enthusiasm as tickets to the circus or a rock concert, remind yourself that this is really very normal. After all, how involved were *you* in the Bible at their age? ("But that's different." No it's not.) The absence of an, *"All right—let's get started!"* doesn't mean your suggestion is doomed to automatic execution on the gallows of secular youth culture.

"The best way out is always through." Here this means communication at its most honest, which is always the most effective way to exorcise ghosts that inhibit good things.

You're right, kids, some parts of the Bible do seem difficult to understand, even a little boring. But the Bible's a big book; we're sure to find something that isn't too deep or too dry. True, we tried it once before and didn't stick with it, but let's give it another shot. We try almost anything more than once, don't we? Yeah, I wasn't always into the Bible myself, but I've learned better and I'd like to share some of it with you—and I know I can learn a lot from you, if we work on it together.

All of this presupposes a real interest on your part (as distinct from a simple hope that if kids read the Bible they won't do drugs), but it doesn't presuppose a vast expertise in Scripture. St. Jerome's comment about the Bible being like a pool is good advice. It's both shallow enough that anyone can jump in and swim without fear of drowning, yet deep enough that the most scholarly can plumb its depths without ever reaching bottom.

Where to Start. So while you need not be armed with scholarly expertise, you do, however, need to supply some structure. Often you can find it ready-made for you in seasonal booklets for Advent or Lent which suggest daily Scripture readings, discussion questions, and activities leading up to the climax of Christmas or Easter. Often these are centered around family mealtime.

This can be a comfortable, natural way to begin, and perhaps more apt to win enthusiasm from children than a bolt out of the parental and scriptural blue. There are many such publications, and quite a few publishers offer new ones each year. Visit your religious bookstore well in advance of the season and check out the possibilities. Some may seem a bit too academic, others a bit too cute or, for whatever reason, just not for you. But you'll find one that looks workable for your family.

Another source of structure for Bible readings can be found in a Christian youth magazine. A month's worth of Bible readings, selected and arranged around a theme (or several), is a regular feature in many of them, and you may find the magazine itself well worth subscribing to for your children. There are many such publications, varying in the age group they're written for—and the scriptural or general religious stance they take (something you would want to check out ahead of time). Again, visit a religious bookstore and see what's available.

Winging It on Your Own. But let's say you're going to wing it on your own—just you, the kids, and the Bible, and you're going to begin ... somewhere. The question is: where? Not with the census and arrangement of the Israelite tribes at the beginning of Numbers, that's for sure. But is there an optimum book, section, chapter, and verse with which to begin for each age group? Of course not. The most certain pieces of advice would be to list a few places *not* to start, such as the above in the Old Testament. Hebrews would be a good place not to begin in the New Testament.

A book or section that you've found personally very meaningful and helpful is a good choice, as long as this doesn't tempt you to monopolize the discussion ("I've read this, and this is what it means") before there *is* any discussion. As long as it doesn't overpower and preclude responses from your children, your own enthusiasm will be contagious.

In the Old Testament, Genesis is a good place to begin. True, there is perhaps more heat generated over chapters 1-11 (the creationism vs. evolution debates, etc.) than over the rest of the Bible put together, but that doesn't make it something to be avoided, especially with older children, who have probably already heard the "But it didn't really happen like that" controversy. A bit of "Well then, what *does* it mean?" can be excellent stimulation for Bible study. You will definitely want to have a general Catholic guide to Scripture for reference with these and many other sections, but remember that this is not a study *task* or a scholarly venture. Or you might want to save those first eleven chapters for later, and start with Genesis 12—the beginning of the great, sweeping story of Abraham's call and the origins of the Israelite people.

An often overlooked Old Testament book is Proverbs, a collection of sometimes profound, sometimes whimsical wisdom, which can be read exactly as it comes—in tiny bits and pieces. Spiritual snack food, so to speak.

Among the Gospels, Matthew is perhaps the best choice for beginners to read straight through (not, for children, at one sitting!), although a case could easily be made for Mark and Luke. John is wonderfully poetic and profound, but not a good choice for children as a New Testament starting point.

The Acts of the Apostles is fun and, for children brought up on a media diet of action-adventure, a good selection. There are no car or even chariot chases in Acts, but it does feature jailbreaks, earthquakes, riots, and shipwrecks as it recounts the early spread of the faith.

Several points are worth noting in conclusion. First, whatever Bible involvement you bring about for your children over and above what is going on now should be counted as progress. Even if it's ten minutes per week, where before there were no minutes per week, that's progress.

Second, as in any human activity, there will be ups and downs—times when Bible reading will be rewarding and times when it will be a little flat. Don't be discouraged by an occasional reaction that's less than ecstatic. Kids who grow to love, let's say, soccer by age sixteen will have commented many times before then about how boring this or that practice (or even game) was. Bible study will not be exempt from such reactions.

Finally, remember that this is not *just* a human activity. God is literally in the words of the Bible—and would like to be involved in our approach to it if we let him do so. It's tempting to think that if we just discover or distill the right *formula* for introducing children to Scripture, it'll work.

As with everything else we do, it's a pretty good idea to pray first and say, "Lead me, Lord." ■

Teaching Little Ones to Pray

Little ones will surprise us with their desire to meet Jesus and to talk to him in prayer.

Patti Mansfield

Years ago when my son Peter was a toddler, I arranged to take my daily prayer time in the afternoon while he watched Sesame Street. One particularly sleepy day I sat in my rocker with the Bible; I kept dozing off. "This will never do," I scolded myself as I got down on my knees. Bending low, hands folded, eyes closed I tried to pray once more. Within a matter of minutes I sensed a presence in the room. No, it wasn't an angel or even an apparition, just my little boy Peter! As I opened my eyes, there he was, crouched down exactly as I was. Peter's nose almost touched mine as he whispered sweetly, "What are we praying about today, Mom?"

This incident spoke volumes to me about teaching small children to pray. Peter not only wanted to be close to me. He wanted to learn to pray. Despite my sleepiness and distractions, my example in prayer was a powerful tool in drawing Peter to seek God, too. I love to picture the child Jesus learning to pray in the home of Mary and Joseph. Surely there must have been times of family prayer, when he observed his earthly parents seeking his heavenly Father.

Our Prayer Life. If we want to teach our small children to pray, it's essential that we be men and women of prayer ourselves. Establish a daily prayer time, if you don't already have one. To communicate the reality of God's love and power to your children, you need to drink daily of the living waters of his presence yourself. Set aside *at least* fifteen minutes of quiet time to pray and read Scripture.

For small children to relate to Jesus in a natural way, they need to understand that he is as close to them as you are. Let your home be permeated by his presence. How can you do this? Most of our relatives live in other states, so we are accustomed to keeping them present to our children through photos, stories, and special visits. In the same way, you can make Jesus a family member by speaking to your little ones about him during the day, reading children's Bible stories at nap time, and having pictures or statues of him in your home.

Above our kitchen table we have a collection of icons and drawings of Jesus, Mary, and the saints, along with a crucifix. Our baby Patrick was not even one year old when he began climbing on a chair to touch the pictures of Jesus and Mary. On many occasions I'd walk into the kitchen and find him kissing and chewing on the corner of the icon of Jesus. "Je, Je," he'd say with enthusiasm as I tried to pry it out of his fingers. In his own little way he was showing honor and love for Jesus. Small children will show their love for God if they are surrounded by reminders of his presence and are encouraged to relate to him. Of course, I would have been happier if Patrick had blown a kiss to Jesus rather than chew on him!

Don't forget the influence of good Christian music in bringing the presence of God to your family. Years ago we used to play Gregorian chants during meals. (The children called it "Agorian Chance.") Recently, we've used more popular Christian music, including delightful children's music tapes. Our two-year-old loves the music of *Psalty the Songbook* and insists on singing and dancing to Christian music almost every day. I'm his favorite dance partner.

Teaching Small Children to Pray. You may teach your little ones both rote prayer and spontaneous prayer. I am amazed at how quickly our young children have been able to memorize prayers such as the "Our Father" and "Hail Mary." My husband has taken the lead in teaching the children these prayers at night before they go to bed. We kneel for a few moments and pray together. Even if they don't understand the meaning of all the words yet, there is a great value in helping our little ones enter into the prayer of the church. I must confess to you that I've only recently learned the ancient prayer called "Soul of Christ." When my four-year-old child committed it to memory, I knew I must too! After our prayers we get in a circle and give a "family hug," which usually ends in giggles.

Spontaneous prayer, talking to Jesus in our own words, is equally as important. Here's where young children are often way ahead of us adults because of their trust. Our youngsters have asked Jesus to do things we didn't have faith for ourselves, and he's answered their prayers.

One day my husband had a headache and our young son Peter, about six at the time, knew it. "I'll pray for you, Dad," offered Peter. He put his hand on his dad's shoulder and said simply, "Jesus, please take Daddy's headache away. Thank you, Jesus." In the next breath he said, "Is it gone, Dad?"

That's faith! When Peter found out the headache was persisting, he persisted and prayed again. Before long, the headache lifted!

Whenever a member of our family is ill or in special need, we try to pray with the laying on of hands. This may be done very simply, yet it has great power in unleashing the healing love of Jesus. My friend's one-year-old hurt her hand and kept holding it out to her mom with the plea, "Or it, or it!" My friend finally realized the child wanted her to pray "over it!" She did and the little one was content. Lay hands in prayer on your children and let them lay hands on you.

Another beautiful way to share prayer with small children is by giving a blessing. One of my most cherished childhood memories is of receiving my mother's blessing at night. She'd trace a small sign of the cross on my forehead. This is a simple but profound way of claiming our children for Christ and marking them with his cross. All our preschoolers have

Suffering and Spine

Life is difficult. Those are three words every thinking human being has had to take in and come to peace with. But that is a fact that at least most middle-class American adolescents are shielded from by well-intentioned parents: that suffering is a natural, unavoidable part of human growth. (Can you imagine, for instance, what life would be like if all the electricity in your house went out for a week?)

That is also part of a father's task, to convince his son or daughter that without legitimate suffering, one remains a petulant child his entire life. The question is not whether life is difficult or not. Difficulty is a given. The question is whether you are going to face suffering honestly and with loved to reverse roles and give us their blessing.

Young children really respond to ceremonies marking the liturgical year within the home. They love the Advent wreath and Jesse tree symbols in preparation for Christmas. For each child's feast day we honor him with a small gift and recall the virtues of his saint. At times we've prayed a novena together as a family for a special intention. Invariably our youngest child will remind us to pray by distributing the prayer cards. He holds his own upside down, but his prayer of babble is powerful nonetheless. Sometimes we pray a decade of the rosary as a family. Again, the smallest child loves to pass out rosary beads to everyone with the command, "Pray!"

Remember to teach your little ones to offer up their sufferings to Jesus. I've been amazed at how quickly young children can grasp this profound concept of redemptive suffering. Let them become familiar with the crucifix by

continued on next page

dignity, or whether you are going to spend your life griping about it or escaping into the anesthesia of booze and drugs or casual sex. If I had to find a single cause for teenage suicides, it would be that teenagers have been misled to expect far more of life and of people than life and people are capable of delivering—like inviting your child to play volleyball in a minefield.

More than a few fathers have said to me, "You know, I made up my mind my kids were never going to have to wade through all the crap I had to when I was young. And, by God, I did it. I gave them everything I never had. But ... you know ... I didn't give them the one thing I got from wading through all that crap: spine."

William J. O'Malley, S.J.

having one in your home. Explain that offering to God our hurts together with Jesus is a form of prayer. One day I reminded my feverish seven-year-old to offer up his sickness. "Oh, Mom, I did that right away," came the reply. If only I could be so quick to unite my sufferings to the cross of Jesus!

A final word about teaching small children to pray. Entrust your family to Mary, the Mother of Jesus and our mother, too. Ask her to wrap her mantle of protection about you as you pass through this life and keep you always close to the heart of her Son, Jesus. She helped form the prayer of the child Jesus. She will surely be a mother to us all by teaching us to pray. ■

A Nest of Catholic Relationships

Building an informal network of Catholic family friends is essential for raising Catholic kids.

John J. Boucher

My wife's best friend calls it the "nesting instinct." By the sixth month of pregnancy with Katie, youngest of five, Therese and I simply had to set up the nursery. We put all our lives on hold in order to build a fitting nest to receive her—putting into place crib, bureau, shelves, clothes, and diapers, like so many twigs and blades of grass.

Though we parents take great care to answer this physical nesting instinct, how often do we prepare a nest of Catholic relationships to receive and nurture our children's faith? In the not-too-distant past such effort was unnecessary, because a family had relationships with other families, friends, and neighbors, who were believers in God and the Catholic faith. But physical and social mobility has exacted a high price on this natural nest of relationships.

Take us for example. Our nuclear family of two adults and five children lives over two hundred miles from our nearest blood relatives. What limited contact we can have with relatives is offset by the fact that many of them are no longer practicing Catholics.

In the absence of closeknit, extended family relationships, here are some ways we have tried to build a network of Catholic friends for our family:

1. *The Witness of Faith-Filled Relatives*. When we travel back home, we carefully select the relatives with which to spend the bulk of our visiting time. Older members of our extended families—grandparents, uncles, and aunts—seem to be the most alive in the faith. So we have made special efforts to bring our children to do things with them.

A special bond has developed between each child and Therese's Great Aunt Lillie. Though ninety-five years old, she continues to live a deep life of faith, which naturally overflows on all of us when we visit her. Whether sharing about the rosaries she has prayed today, about watching daily Mass on TV, or about the pizza party she wants to throw in celebration of our visit, Aunt Lillie witnesses to the living God.

2. *Getting to Know Priests, Sisters, and Lay Ministers*. We have established the custom of inviting priests, sisters, and lay ministers to our house periodically for supper. As a result, church leaders are real persons to our children and not just spiritual authority figures. Even our teens feel comfortable around those who serve us in the church. Our youth trust them and readily bring questions and problems to them.

3. Godparents as Role Models. We have attempted to choose with great care each child's godparents for baptism. This has been a tremendous challenge. It's nearly impossible to know if godparents will be in contact with our children when we move from one part of the country to another. Moreover, will they continue practicing their faith throughout the life of their godchildren? Will they be available to our youth when faith questions and doubts arise?

Timothy's godfather, Dan, has been a close family friend for years. He not only shares his Catholic beliefs with Tim when he visits. He lives and shares his love of God and the church with all of our children. Confidently, Therese and I decided to ask him to be little Katie's godfather, too.

4. Adoptive Grandparents, Uncles, and Aunts. We have learned it's possible to adopt foster grandparents, uncles, and aunts in each new location to serve as Catholic faith

Choosing Role Models for Your Kids

As parents we want our kids to follow Jesus and pattern their lives on his. But to become like Christ, children need flesh and blood role models who show them how to live as he would right now in their world. In my youth ministry, I have found young Catholic adults—men and women in their early twenties—to be invaluable models for teens. Where parishes or groups involve them in this kind of service, you find that high school youth stay active, stay involved, and stay in love with Jesus and the church.

Most young adults I know are usually very eager to share and give. When invited to help with younger kids, they respond with zeal, enthusiasm, and commitment. Since they seem to thrive on challenge, I say enlist them in models. When Katie was born, our friend June assumed the role of honorary grandmother. Jerry, another senior citizen, became an honorary grandfather. Both of them have willingly extended their love and faith support to our older children as well. We make a special point to get together with one or another of them each month.

5. Holding Home Bible Studies. At different times Therese and I have held weekly or biweekly Catholic Bible studies in our home. Though young children aren't interested in such study, teenagers often are. Encouraging our children to socialize with participants before or after the meetings has been a good way for them to develop relationships with believing adults.

6. Taking Advantage of Religious Education Programs. One of the most powerful religious influences in our children's
continued on next page

---

the tough job of keeping our kids Catholic.

When we are trying to find young adults to relate to our kids, there are other important qualities to look for. The more these are in place, the more you can be sure they will influence your youngsters for good:

1. Commitment to Christ. Have they decided to follow Jesus? Do they spend time praying daily?

2. Understanding the Catholic faith. Do they know the basics of Catholic doctrine and practice? Do they make use of the sacraments?

3. Positive Self-image. Are they thankful for who they are and what God has given them? Are they happy with who they are in their own eyes and the eyes of others?

4. Healthy Peer Relationships. Do they conform more
continued on next page

lives between ages four and thirteen has been our involvement with family religious education programs in local parishes. Though the structure of these programs has varied, the following elements are generally present: large group worship, classes for each age group, adult study group, family art projects, and suggested family home activities to reinforce the theme studied over the following weeks.

Family religious education serves as an excellent alternative or as a supplement to weekly religion classes for children. Ask your parish religious education director or the diocesan office of religious education/catechesis for guid-

---

readily to Christian values than to the pressures of their peers?

5. *Good Family Relationships.* Do they relate well to their parents and brothers and sisters?

6. *Service.* Do they give themselves generously in serving others?

7. *Community.* Do they share their life with others?

Of course you cannot expect perfection of role models, but you should be relatively sure that they are moving in the right direction in most of these areas.

At a time when communication often breaks down between parents and teenagers—and when teens are looking for ways to distance themselves from parents to establish their own identity—young Catholic adults can play an important role. Not only can they help families relate better, linking parents and teens, but by their joyful service they can get kids to accept Christian values. I say let's put them to work.

Tim Briffett

ance in starting family religious education in your area if it is not already available.

7. Meeting Regularly with Another Catholic Family. Monthly informal gatherings with another Catholic family has helped provide a strong network of faith relationships for our children. We have tried to plan a meal or special outing (museum trip, walk to the park, taking in a movie, and so on) with a family whose children are roughly the same age as ours. However, we have found that is not

---

Older members of our extended families seem to be the most alive in the faith. We have made special efforts to bring our children to do things with them.

---

absolutely necessary. What is necessary is that adults in both families treat each child as a unique person, asking personal questions about daily matters, then listening carefully and responding.

In today's society, providing a nest or network of Catholic relationships for the nurturing of our children in the faith is not a optional extra. It is as important as the nest we make to receive our young at birth, and it takes considerable planning and effort. For your success at this loving task, I join my prayers with those of St. Paul, "For this reason I kneel before the Father, from whom every family in heaven and on earth is named, that he may grant you in accord with the riches of his glory to be strengthened with power through his Spirit ...." (Eph 3:14-16). ∎

Think, Act, & Pray

FAMILY FUN NIGHT

FOR REFLECTION AND DISCUSSION

1. Why should families worship together at Mass? (See article by the Eastons.)
2. What can parents do to teach children the value of going to confession? (See article by the Vandagriffs.)
3. How can we begin to study the Bible together as a family? (See article by Auer.)
4. What are some techniques for teaching little children to pray? (See article by Mansfield.)
5. What are some ways we can develop relationships with individuals and other families? (See articles by Boucher and Briffett.)

TAKING STOCK

1. Review the decisions you have made to help keep your children Catholic. The following inventory will help you:
    a. What decisions did you make to draw closer to God yourself? Have you followed through on them faithfully?
    b. Have you started praying daily for your family?
    c. Have you initiated family prayer? Have you kept at it?
    d. What other decisions did you make? Have you implemented them?

2. Which of the following practices suggested in this chapter does your family do?
    —worship together at Mass
    —participate in the sacrament of reconciliation
    —study the Bible together
    —teach children private prayer
    —build relationships with other Catholics

PLAN FOR ACTION

Select one practice from those suggested in this chapter and implement it in your family. Use the article that presents the practice as a guide.

ACTIVITY

Family Fun Night. Plan an evening of family games to celebrate a birthday or Christian holiday. You could view it as an experiment which, if it works, could be introduced as a regular part of your family life. You might want to include some of the following elements:

- Involve everyone in planning different parts of the evening.
- Start off with a little nicer meal than usual and be sure to have dessert. (Consider reserving dessert to wrap up the night.)
- Begin with simple prayers before meals. If you decide that this is the only chance for prayer, you might make it a little more elaborate than usual. You could read a short Scripture, possibly the first reading from next Sunday's Mass, and have everybody say what it brings

to mind. You could also go from person to person, having everyone thank God out loud for something he's done for them.

- Select a number of games. Be sure someone knows how to explain the rules and that you have assembled everything you need in advance (unless you plan a scavenger hunt).

- If you do not have a longer prayer time to start, end with one. You might consider a little Scripture sharing and then a thanksgiving prayer. Close the night with the Our Father, a Hail Mary, and a Glory Be.

- You can expect a little uneasiness from teenagers who are not accustomed to family activities. Be patient. Most will come to enjoy such events.

- In the future, consider inviting young single adults or another Catholic family to join you for a family fun night.

RESOURCES

Mass and Sacraments

- *The Children's Mass Book* (Regina Press).
- *Together at Mass* A Child's Mass Book (Ave Maria Press).
- *My First Mass Book* (Regina Press).
- Francine O'Connor, *The ABC's of the Sacraments for Children* (Our Sunday Visitor).
- Mickey and Terri Quinn, *How to Interest Your Children in the Mass* (Liturgical Press).
- Peter M. J. Stravinskas, *The Bible and the Mass* (Servant).
- Peter M. J. Stravinskas, *Understanding the Sacraments* (Servant).

Bible Study

(See also **Resources** for chapter four.)

- *The Bible in Pictures for Little Eyes* (Moody Press).
- *The Catholic Children's Bible* (Regina Press).
- *New Catholic Picture Bible* (Catholic Bible Press).
- Jim Auer, *A Teenager's (Absolutely Basic) Introduction to the New Testament* (Liguori).
- George A. Martin, *Reading Scripture as the Word of God* (Servant).
- Marilyn Norquist, *How to Pray and Read the Gospels* (Liguori).
- See Jim Auer's video program, "The Bible: What's It All About" (2 cassettes; 360 minutes), which is available from Fransciscan Communications, 1229 S. Santee St., Los Angeles, CA 90015.

Celebrating the Church Year

(See also **Resources** for chapter four.)

- Joan Halmo, *Celebrating the Church Year with Young Children* (Liturgical Press).
- Daniel L. Lowery, C.S.S.R., *Day by Day Through Lent: Reflections, Prayers, Practices* (Liguori).

SIX

Keeping Teenagers Close to Christ

*Developing strong relationships and good communi-
cation with your teens helps them develop a strong
relationship and good communication with God.*

Talk with Your Teenager

*Our parental role requires us to take the lead
in having good communication with
our teenage children.*

Bert Ghezzi

"Do you know what I am?" a teenage boy once asked.
"I'm a comma. Whenever I talk to my dad, he stops talking
and makes a comma. Then when I stop talking, he starts
right up again as if I didn't say anything. I'm just a comma in
the middle of his speeches." Counselor Jay Kesler quoted
this boy in a book on parent-teen communications called
How to Get Your Teenager to Talk to You.

Chances are that if we could ask that boy's dad about his
relations with his son, he would say they communicate just

fine. Like many parents, he may be unaware of the communication breakdown between him and his teenager. The book cited above reports the results of a study conducted at Michigan State University on communications between 3,000 teens and their parents. Seventy-nine percent of the parents said they were communicating with their teenagers. However, 81 percent of the teens interviewed said that their parents were not communicating with them.

Teens' Complaints. Recently I attended a youth meeting in my parish to ask a dozen typical Catholic teenagers about their communication with their moms and dads. It was an ear-opening visit, and I told them that what they said made me determined to do better with my own kids. Here is a short list of their complaints about parents' failures in communicating:

- **Put-downs:** "When my dad doesn't approve of something I've done, he puts me down by saying things like

What Teens Want from Parents

When teenagers are asked how their parents can improve communication with them, here's what they most often say:

1. "Be accessible. Listen when we talk. You don't know how hard it may have been for us to come to you. Allow us to express our opinions even if they disagree with yours."
2. "Be reasonable in establishing rules and flexible in enforcing them (sometimes our excuses are sincere

'Can't you ever do anything right?' or 'Are all seventeen-year-olds just naturally stupid?' "

- **Clamming Up:** "If my mother doesn't like where a discussion is going, she says, 'Enough! We're not going to talk about it any more!' and she, like, plugs her ears."
- **Hidden Agendas:** "We can be talking about one thing, but then all of a sudden my dad shifts gears and gets on my case for something else that's been bugging him."
- **Stonewalling:** "The worst thing my parents do is: if I ask permission to do something and they say no, and I ask them why, they say 'because.' "
- **Just Plain Not Listening:** "My mom doesn't listen to what I'm saying, which causes me to not really hear her."

When I am in a defensive mood, I can pick out similar flaws in my teenagers. Undeniably it takes two to tangle, and teens contribute their fair share to communication difficulties. However, life circumstances tend to excuse

continued on next page

ones). If you need to punish us, please be consistent and fair."

3. "Let us make mistakes—we'll learn from them. But when we do make a mistake, hold off on the 'I told you so!' "
4. "Affirm that we are loved, even when we don't deserve it. We don't always like ourselves either. We know when we've goofed up—and your patience and support are so important."
5. "Be an example to us of mature, growing Christians. We know our faith has to be our own, but we need strong role models to help us pattern our lives."

Karen Heffner

them, and to lay the bulk of the responsibility for maintaining good communication on us parents.

If teens are withdrawn, testy, and otherwise uncommunicative, sometimes it may be that they're just being bad. Often, however, their adolescence makes them do it. Physiological and psychological changes, insecurity, identity crises, confusion, and immaturity—all limit their relational skills. Circumstances challenge parents, too, but they just don't get us off the hook. Our parental role requires us to take the lead in communicating with our teenage children.

Steps to Take. There are steps parents can take that will bring an immediate measure of improvement to their relations with their teenage children. Here are three that I find most helpful:

- **Stop, Look, Listen:** When teenagers want to talk, give them your undivided attention. *Stop* whatever you are doing—close your book, turn off the television, interrupt your chore. *Look* at the youth while he or she is speaking to you; good eye contact helps communication (and keeps you from getting distracted). *Listen* to what your teens are saying, and try to see their point of view. Let them know you are taking what they say seriously.
- **Explain:** Be willing to give reasons for your decisions, otherwise be prepared to be viewed as unreasonable, for so you will appear to be. When we can't give explanations or reasons other than "because I'm the father, that's why," we ought to be sure we are not acting out of pique or out of disregard for our teens.
- **Minimize Potential for Conflict:** One of the best ways I know to reduce conflict between parent and teenager is to have a few clearly established rules that are consistently applied. For example, Mary Lou and I have always had a short list of punishable offenses:

deliberate disobedience, lying, willfully hurting someone, and violating the curfew. Punishments for viola-
tions are defined in advance and tailored to the
teenager. This approach works if rules are clear, kept to
a minimum, explained thoroughly, and applied consistently. They work best when parents listen as their kids
explain their view of an alleged infraction, and are
gracious enough to be flexible when necessary.

There are, however, some deeper currents, like under-
tows, that can force breakdowns in our relations with our
teens. If we learn to deal with such issues as time, anger, and
fear, we will make long-term, appreciable progress.

Not Enough Time. Failure to invest sufficient time is a prime
cause of communication breakdowns. Dad gets too busy
with work or becomes too involved in a hobby and has very
little time to relate to the kids. So he takes short cuts: he
doesn't want any unnecessary discussion; he says he'll talk
about it later, but later never comes; he saves time by doing
something else while talking. I am speaking here as an
insider. For example, I have had to endure with great
embarrassment my sixteen-year-old son Peter's devastating
impersonation of me going off to another room while some
family member is talking to me.

If we are stingy with time toward our kids, the real issue
may be our selfishness. We can easily put behind us the
youthful generosity we had as new parents, and put our
own interests ahead of relating to our children. Once when I
was spending every spare moment writing a book, a
thought demanded my attention, and I'm sure it came from
God: "You're devoting yourself to a book that will last about
ten years, and neglecting children who will live forever."
From that time I have tried to keep my priorities right,
investing more in my family than in my avocation. I
renewed that resolve ten years later on the day the

publisher notified me that they were letting my book go out of print.

Handling Our Anger. Anger plays a big role in undermining good parent-teenager communication. For example, discussions with Mom seem to escalate immediately into shouting matches, because of her accumulated frustrations. Dad thinks he detects a defiant attitude that challenges him, so he is on his teenager's back for every little thing.

Anger can be constructive if we direct it only at behavior that is seriously wrong—not at the teenager himself. I once sat a teen down and said with great emotion, "You know that I love you, and that's why I am furious about what you have done!" Anger carefully aimed can support the child in eliminating bad conduct. However, expressing strong anger over inconveniences or frustrated personal preferences is wasted energy and may be destructive of good rela-

Sticking to a Few Rules—Flexibly

Our kids live in a world of blinding change, filled with many more choices than we faced. They are exposed to moral, ethical, and religious ideas which were only hinted at in earlier, simpler days. We can't change what the world offers, but we can help our teens by reducing the number of choices they need to make as members of our family.

Anna, my wife, and I require all of our kids to participate in a few regular family practices, which assure us of opportunities to pass on our religious heritage. We expect everyone to attend Sunday Mass, to be at family meals, and to participate in family prayer.

tionships. I once blew up because a clumsy teen accidentally broke a TV dial. Later I heard him say, "We all had to suffer just because Dad was inconvenienced." He was right; I apologized.

The Problem of Insecurity. Insecurity makes some parents communicate poorly with their teenagers. For example, parents who refuse to discuss things or give explanations may do so because they are afraid of failure. They fear that their teens will get into trouble with bad friends and drugs. They fear that their kids won't obey them. They fear their kids will end up as bad adults. And they fear that God will hold them accountable for all this failure. Ironically, the fear itself generates conduct that can make their fears come true. However, if we parents can keep things in the right perspective, we will be freer to relate better to our kids. First, the Lord does not hold us responsible for our children's

continued on next page

Developing a Strategy. Since adolescents naturally battle most efforts at adult direction, we need to choose where we will bend and where we will not. Once they know what is not negotiable, there is a better chance that they will even accept and begin to like the practice. However, a little flexibility wisely applied can help teens conform to our expectations. I have learned, for example, that sometimes a child is not resisting Mass attendance as much as he resents looking like a kid being dragged to church with his parents. So now and then I allow a child to attend Mass separately or with friends. And as it gets harder to have nightly meals together, we expect our young adults to phone if they are going to miss supper. A little flexibility helps our family stick to the rules.

Robert R. Iatesta

salvation. He will judge them, not us, for whatever they do, bad or good. Second, being a good parent means doing the very best we can and trusting God that our children will turn out right.

I learned an important lesson here from my mother. When my dad died in 1953, she began to raise four children ranging in age from five months to twelve years, and she did it as a single parent. I know she had her worries about us. But every night she knelt at her bedside and prayed for each of us.

If we want to communicate well with our teenagers, we should communicate with God about them. ∎

Getting Our Teens to Talk to Us

*Affection is the oil and forgiveness the repair kit
that keep family communication in good working order.
And understanding is a rearview mirror
that keeps things in perspective.*

Bert Ghezzi

"What is another word for 'monosyllabic'?", I had asked.

"John," answered my daughter Clare, then four years old. Her eyes flashed, because she knew we were teasing her brother. My son John, then sixteen years old, was at the stage of adolescence that requires teens to speak to parents only when necessary, and then only in one-syllable words. One at a time, of course.

Mary Lou and I have five children who are now or have

been teens, and two more are still coming down the pike. Getting them to talk to us has never been easy. Even those who are talkative as children clam up when puberty strikes. Funny how those hormones that cause everything else to grow seem to retard speech. However, overall our communication with our adolescents seems to have been modestly successful.

My wife is better at getting our teenagers to talk than I am. Mary Lou is a good listener and she is patient. She has always carried on informal conversations with our teens about subjects that interested them—sports, music, movies, and other important youth-culture topics. She makes herself inconspicuously available when she suspects they might be untypically voluble. When she senses something is wrong, she probes with questions. She's accessible and understanding, so they end up talking to her.

I also have good conversations with our teens, but fewer. I could kid myself that just being the father causes a certain distance that impedes communication. That's true, as far as it goes. However, the whole truth is that I'm impatient and impetuous: I come down too hard, too quickly. So the kids have found me somewhat difficult to talk to. Consequently, I have had to work at it, with results that have been sometimes satisfactory, sometimes not.

There are some long-standing patterns in our family life that have made communication with our teens somewhat easier. These are expressing affection, asking forgiveness, and trying to be understanding.

I Love You. Early in our marriage Mary Lou and I learned the value of frequently telling the children that we loved them. Also we have routinely encouraged them to express their affection to us and to each other. Of course, I find it easier to say "I love you" to seven-year-old Mary, who always seems perky and helpful, than to my teenagers, who do not. However, I do personally express my love for them and so does Mary Lou.

We like the teenagers to express affection, too, but they seem to prefer to show it rather than to say it. Once, for example, I noticed that the family room and hallway carpet had been mysteriously vacuumed. I asked how it happened, and Mary Lou said Stephen, then age seventeen, had done it without being asked. He was saying "I love you" to his mother.

Our openly expressed affection has encouraged communication with our teens. Because they know our love for them, they find it somewhat easier to talk to us. However, don't get the wrong idea that conversation at our house flows as easily as it does for the Huxtables on "The Cosby Show" and for other ideal TV families. It doesn't. We have plenty of rough spots that stem from flaws in the parents as well as the teens.

I Forgive You. Another practice that Mary Lou and I learned early has helped to get us through conflicts and to repair

Creating Chances for Conversations

Now and then we have spontaneous conversations with our kids. That's actual grace. More often communicating with them requires work. In different seasons of our family's life, Mary Lou and I have used a variety of means to facilitate communication with our older children. We built into our family schedule opportunities for everyone to communicate, especially to speak about themselves. Some of these have been just informal times together, and some have been times designated formally for communication. Here is a sampler:

• "My Day." For nearly a decade, during the evening meal everyone was expected to tell about the highlights of their day. After everyone had a chance to share, communications when they break down. When members of the family offend another by something they say or do, we expect them to ask forgiveness. If one of our teenage boys, for example, loses his "cool" and strikes another child, he must fix the breach by saying "I was wrong. Please forgive me." And we also expect aggrieved parties to forgive quickly, even if they don't feel like it. Oh, yes, the policy holds for Dad and Mom, too. For example, if I let my anger get in control of me, which happens more often than I like to admit, I ask forgiveness of anyone I may offend in the process, even teenage sons.

I Understand You. We have tried to make our teenagers feel at home with us, even when they seem to have become perfect strangers. Our efforts at putting ourselves in their shoes is the fruit of Mary Lou's ability to understand what's really going on. When a teenager is moody and withdrawn, for example, I'm inclined to go in like gangbusters to turn

continued on next page

---

we wrapped up with a round of spontaneous prayer. We still laugh at the memory of Elaine at age four sharing "my day" in unbearably repetitive detail.

- *Family Night.* At times we have designated a certain night for the family to be together just to have fun. Mary Lou prepared a nice dinner to launch "family night." The evening usually involved activities such as games, singing, viewing a movie, attending a ball game, or the like. Often there were guests; always there was dessert.

- *The Snack.* Once I scheduled a nightly "snack" at 9 P.M., when all would gather for light food and conversation. No one was supposed to eat anything after dinner. I was trying to capitalize on the constant hunger of adolescents. The snack worked moderately well for about a year, then we shifted to other ways of keeping conversation going.

continued on next page

them around. Occasionally, that's not a bad approach. But when I manage to take my time and consult Mary Lou, I often learn she has discerned several factors behind the behavior that call for a more delicate technique. And when we can recall the confusion and insecurity of our adolescence, we are a little more patient with our adolescents.

Mary Lou and I also work at understanding the youth culture that competes with us for our teenagers' hearts. We have decided to appreciate whatever we can in it and take issue only with those things that plainly contradict our Christian values. For example, we listen to our teens' music and have even taken them to carefully selected rock concerts. That way we can talk to them about their music, pointing out the good and the bad. We hope such conversations will teach them some discernment.

Expressing affection is the oil and asking forgiveness is the repair kit that together keep our family's communication in relatively good working order. And trying to be understanding is a rearview mirror that keeps things in perspective.

Currently, our family communication is unstructured, because Mary Lou and I are home most evenings and can

---

• *The Appointment.* When my evenings fill up with meetings, I schedule regular weekly appointments with the teenage children. We often take a long walk, stop at an ice cream parlor, or just go out for a Coke. At these times I ask leading questions about school, their friends, their current interests. I bring up problems they are having with us or we are having with them. And they have a chance to raise their concerns, too.

Bert Ghezzi

spend time with the children who are still with us. Every day we try to have several conversations with our teens, Stephen (nineteen) and Peter (sixteen). As always, I have to use more words than they, but we seem to understand each other. Weekdays I have breakfast with our daughters Clare (twelve) and Mary (seven). Then I drive them to school, and we never stop talking. Hard to believe, but it won't be long before Clare herself will be "monosyllabic." But I expect the daily time we are investing in communication will produce future benefits in our relationship.

I already know the effort pays off. Some of the best conversations I have now are with my daughter Elaine, age twenty, my son Paul, age twenty-two, and John, who is twenty-four and no longer monosyllabic. ∎

Breaking Through to Teens

At sixteen I stopped believing in God. But a few years later, through the witness of some friends, I came to know Jesus and I returned to the Catholic church.

David Farmer

I'll never forget the look on my mother's face when I told her I no longer believed in God.

For all of my sixteen years she and my father had prayed faithfully for me. They saw to it that I attended Sunday Mass and religious education classes, and asked God to bless the food before meals. But, as far as I was concerned, Mass was utterly boring, and confirmation was more of a graduation from church than a commitment to embrace it as an adult. An eloquent lecture given by my favorite high school teacher on the absurdity of religion sealed the issue. He believed humanity could make the world a better place on its own, and I embraced his humanistic views.

During the following years I carried on as most of my friends. I was involved in various sports, played the trombone, and applied myself to my studies. Occasionally my buddies and I were caught drinking or skipping class, but overall we were considered "good kids."

Beneath my cool, contented guise, however, was an insecure teenager. I was overly self-conscious of my dental braces and acne. I often was on the verge of depression, feeling lonely and misunderstood.

Theory or Reality? Is God's desire to reach youth merely a pipe dream? For many parents of spiritually lukewarm teenagers, it may seem so. This must have been the frame of mind my parents were in as I left for the University of Michigan at the age of eighteen.

When some new acquaintances invited me to have dinner with them the week I arrived on campus, I accepted, not knowing I would leave with more than a full stomach.

At that meal I encountered something I had never encountered before: joyful Christians. I saw people my own age affirming one another in a natural, relaxed way. Their brief prayer before dinner was spontaneous and personal, and they were genuinely interested in me, a mere freshman! They were intelligent, secure, and—much to my amazement—several of the guys looked athletic as well. My image of the weak and fainthearted Christian was completely destroyed. I wasn't yet convinced God was real, but I could no longer dismiss the possibility.

Driven by a desire for the happiness these Christians had, I began my search for God. I asked him to reveal himself to me, yet I refused to give up my old ways. Seven months later my Christian friends challenged me to stop leading a double life, to choose for or against Christ, to live the life of a believer or to quit associating with them altogether. That was all it took.

I committed my life to God. Soon I was baptized in the Holy Spirit and began to experience a release from the loneliness I felt—I had a Father in heaven who cared for me and was accessible. At eighteen my life took on new meaning and direction.

I had found God, but I hadn't found a church. My past experience with Catholicism left me cold. I figured I would just keep attending the campus prayer meetings where God was so obviously present.

Soon, though, a friend I respected told me I should find a church where I could receive the sacraments and grow in my understanding of God. So off I went each Sunday morning to a different church. I couldn't say exactly what I was looking for. But I knew I wasn't finding it.

Weeks later—in my dorm room, of all places—I finally found what I was seeking. It was there that a priest took the time to explain Catholicism to me in a way that I could actually understand. Suddenly the Eucharist and papal infallibility, Marian devotion and the teaching authority of the church, didn't seem absurd. In fact, they made a lot of sense. They were God's provision for me, helps to get me to heaven. And they were *real.*

This is only one way the Catholic church has broadened my understanding of reality. But that isn't all. Its ancient wisdom continually helps me make sense of my life, even the suffering. Most of all, though, the church has nurtured my personal relationship with God.

My life still has its problems, but it is so much better now that God is with me and I am with him. And all he did by revealing himself to me, he deepened by leading me back to the Catholic church.

Not Alone. As a teenager my situation was typical. Most of my friends, even those who attended the local Catholic high school, tell similar tales. We all seemed to be fumbling our way through high school with little peace of mind and declining morals. If we could skip Mass on Sunday, we would.

Recent Gallup polls tell us we were not alone. They report that six out of ten Catholic adolescents fail to attend Mass, while five out of six condone premarital sex. A prominent researcher from the Catholic University of America predicts that one out of five Catholic girls now age fourteen will become pregnant during their high school years.

This is not to say that most of my friends, or Catholic teens in general, deny the reality of the spiritual realm. In fact, according to Gallup, 95 percent of America's teenagers believe in the existence of God. And if those who disbelieve are anything like me, then their disbelief does not signify a

The Good Father

The good father is the man who patterns his life on the Father before whom all of us are children. Our Father doesn't fight our battles for us, but he's always there, urging us on, if we allow him to. And he never tires of listening to us. And he rarely interrupts. But if we make ourselves vulnerable to him, we hear what every son yearns to hear: "You are my son, in whom—no matter what—I am well pleased."

Perhaps the first step for a father—no matter the cost of embarrassment to him or his child—is God's consistent way with Israel: to get him (or her) off into a place alone. Then, to put his arms around the child and say, "Son (or daughter), I know we both screw up sometimes. But I love you. God, how I do love you."

It's worth a try.

William J. O'Malley, S.J.

lack of openness to God, but rather a lack of experience of true Christian fellowship.

Sadly, we must conclude that Catholic youth are generally aware of spiritual reality but usually don't find religious education, weekly Mass, and their Catholic education spiritually fulfilling. They fall away from the church to search in vain for happiness elsewhere.

God's Plan? Surprisingly, some people accept this teenage falling away as if it were part of a natural process of maturation, or as if it somehow were God's plan for teens to lose interest in the church, perhaps to return one day, perhaps not.

It is not God's desire for young people to leave the church. No father desires a beloved child to run away from home. Rather, God desires that none of his little ones should be lost (see Matthew 18:14).

God intends, rather, that teenagers be examples of faith and righteousness. St. Paul exhorts Timothy, "Let no one have contempt for your youth, but set an example for those who believe, in speech, conduct, love, faith, and purity" (1 Tm 4:12). St. John addresses young men in his first letter: "... You are strong, and the word of God remains in you, and you have conquered the evil one" (1 Jn 2:14).

Similarly, the Catholic church has high expectations for her youth. Pope Paul VI in "On Evangelization in the Modern World," says, "Young people who are well trained in faith and prayer must become more and more the apostles of youth. The Church counts greatly on their contribution" (No. 72).

John Paul II once encouraged youth in a speech at Madison Square Garden: "The Church needs you. The world needs you because it needs Christ.... And so I ask you to accept your responsibility in the Church: to help—by your words and, above all, by the example of your lives—to spread the gospel."

Like me, your young men and women are waiting for the challenge of a real and lively faith. ■

Ten Tips for
Teaching Teens to Pray

Yes, teenagers may ask about prayer,
and may even let you teach them how.
So, be prepared with these proven ways.

Joseph Moore

How are we to deal in everyday life with teenagers' questions about the effectiveness of prayer? To accompany our young people on a journey of faith requires a great deal of personal contact. Adults need to listen to the teenagers' personal experiences as they grow up. They need to review with them how their prayer is articulated, offer encouragement, and help them reshape their prayer in mature terms. By reflecting with adolescents on the nature of their prayer, adults can make brief comments which help expand the horizon of how to pray and what to pray for.

Here are ten tips for teaching teens to pray:

1. Keep It Simple. Sometimes when we try to explain spirituality or suggest methods of prayer, we intimidate young people without realizing it. Affirm what works for them. Don't encumber them with a lot of spiritual vocabulary. You might make them feel a relationship with God is for the chosen few.

Simplicity is at the heart of spirituality. This doesn't mean we can naively ignore complexities. It does mean that, amid noise and materialistic values, we need to cling to our deepest human and religious values. Simplification implies

Encourage youths to find a specific time to pray each day, even if it is brief. Help them see that any friendship requires spending time with the friend.

stripping away what is useless, harmful, or needlessly burdensome.

2. Discuss the Youth's Concept of God (or Jesus). Is God close? Is God warm or cold, concerned or not? Is God a judge or a vague reality? A parent or a friend? And where is God—in church, in heaven, in one's heart, in other people? There are no right or wrong answers to these questions, but asking them helps. You may unearth some childish notions: God as a sort of police officer, for example. In this case, point to God's total acceptance of each of us.

3. Suggest Regular Prayer. Encourage youths to find a specific time to pray each day, even if it is brief. (Five to ten minutes is sufficient.) Help them see that any friendship requires spending time with the friend. So too with Jesus. That's what prayer is: developing the friendship.

Encourage them also to have a specific place to pray. Some find it helpful to create a "prayer corner" or special place to pray with a special mat or rug on which to sit or kneel.

Lighting a candle or incense helps create the mood or environment. Playing a mellow song as a preamble can help teenagers unwind. But ask them to turn the radio or stereo off for at least a few moments of real silence. The prophet

Elijah in the Old Testament found that God was not to be found in the loud wind or the earthquake or the fire, but rather in a soft whisper (see 1 Kings 19:12).

4. Introduce New Prayer Forms. Scripture is an excellent source of spiritual nourishment for young people. The Gospels are so concrete. If a youngster finds it difficult to spend five or ten minutes a day in prayer without day-dreaming, recommend a short Gospel section for reflecting on how it applies to the teen's personal life. This type of reflecting is called meditation.

Another form of prayer more alien to our hectic Western society is contemplation. First of all, it requires that we be totally relaxed and that we turn all our interior motors off. Our society is so geared to activity and achievement that it is very hard for most of us just to be still.

The most important thing is to turn off mind activity, memory, imagination. Contemplation is quite different from meditation, which relies on the mind's activity. Contemplation is a simple attempt to be still and know God. It is the experience of love itself. Meditation resembles two friends in conversation, while contemplation resembles two people who know each other so well that they can just gaze at each other and feel intense love.

Contemplative experiences cannot be forced. Sometimes they just happen—for example, when we are overcome by the roaring of the sea or the beauty of a sunset. The effect of nature is so profound that we suspend our thought processes, if only for a few moments. This can also happen in prayer—we can be so overwhelmed by an experience of God's love that we just bask in that feeling without having any thoughts.

Generally this form of prayer is a gift to those who have been faithful for some time to daily meditation. I would not recommend it right away to a teen unless he or she is experienced in prayer.

5. *Recommend Asceticism.* That harsh-sounding word comes from a Greek word meaning "to exercise." It refers not to prayer but to preparation.

Asceticism implies the self-control to shut the door for at least a short while from the noisy confusion of the world. It means having the self-discipline to turn off the radio and take the phone off the hook for fifteen minutes so prayer can proceed undisturbed. Asceticism means that we choose to sit upright rather than stretch out on a couch in order to be fully attentive to communication with God. Asceticism also means we spend the amount of time we have promised ourselves, no matter how many distractions come our way.

Diet and physical exercise are also ascetic practices. It's hard to focus our communication on a purely spiritual level if we have a too-full stomach or are feeling the effect of caffeine or sugar or some other substance. The more balanced and nutritious our diet, the more we will feel prepared to turn to prayer. So too with exercise. Exercise tunes our bodies and clears our minds so we are able more easily to turn to God in prayer.

6. *Encourage Journal Keeping.* A good habit is keeping a daily journal of the Spirit's movements. A journal helps us focus on our relationship with God and will indicate areas where growth is needed or the directions in which God is calling. If your youngster is willing to share what he or she has written, it can serve as a springboard to conversation about prayer.

7. *Define Genuine Religious Experience.* Sometimes certain phenomena are mistaken by youth as spiritual experiences—the peaceful feeling induced by marijuana, for example. Here are a few criteria for discerning a real spiritual experience. If a young person describes something that you don't feel is genuinely religious, check out your hunch against these points adapted from *The Practice of Spiritual Direction* by William A. Barry and William J. Connolly:

- Does it seem like a religious experience? Does it compare to previous experiences of which you are certain? Is it consistent with what you know of God or Jesus?
- Is it honest? (This may be difficult to sort out with adolescents because they have such a jumble of intense feelings.)
- Is it characterized by a genuine sense of peace? Does it bring calm to the spirit?
- Are all the fruit of the Spirit present?

Our young people are growing up in a culture that relies very little upon God.

---

8. Don't Be Afraid of Doubt. In a technological age where we can do so many things ourselves, God's primacy can be overshadowed. Our young people are growing up in a culture that relies very little upon God. Coupled with this is another phenomenon: the crisis of faith that used to be common in early adulthood often occurs during late adolescence. Does God exist? This question usually rises from the more sensitive, reflective young person.

9. Don't Over-react. This crisis is normal. It is common now that faith has so few cultural supports. Faith, we must always remember, is a gift from God—not something we can manufacture.

If young people are seeking the meaning of life and ultimate reality, we have to wait quietly and patiently until they are gifted by a new and more profound awareness of

Jesus Christ. If they honestly confront their own inner emptiness, they will eventually discover that only God can fill them up.

10. Talk about Sunday Liturgy. Young teenagers often oppose attendance at Mass as a way of testing parental limits. Discerning the difference between this testing and a real crisis of faith can be thorny. Here are some possible directions to take:

- No matter how much you disagree, try to listen patiently to a teenager's objection. Feeling heard is, in all probability, half the issue. In faith, we need to show deep respect for another's viewpoint, even if the other is young. We can't lose sight of Jesus' message—an invitation, not a command. We need to reflect on Christ's attitude.

- Explore parish opportunities for teenagers to work on the liturgy with people their age. Would that be of help in deriving more fulfillment from attendance?

- Realize that most spiritual formation occurs in the family. Most youngsters learn religious practices in the home; and if they reject them for a time, there is a high probability that they will readopt them in the future. Leave it to God and don't be distressed.

- Share your reasons for attending Mass. The Eucharist is a most precious gift. Your own appreciation of that gift will say much more to young people than your words. When the rich young man refused to follow (Mk 10:17-23), Jesus did not coerce him to a Christian lifestyle. We must always remember that Jesus is our model for inviting young men and women to follow him. ■

Think, Pray, & Act

IMPROVING FAMILY COMMUNICATION

FOR REFLECTION AND DISCUSSION

1. What are some of the main obstacles to good communication between parents and teenagers? What can be done to overcome them? (See articles by Ghezzi and Heffner.)
2. What can parents do to get their teens to talk to them? (See article by Ghezzi.)
3. What steps can parents take to improve relationships with their teenagers? (See articles by Ghezzi and Iatesta.)
4. How can we bring teenage children closer to Christ? (See articles by Farmer and Moore.)

TAKING STOCK

Assess the state of communication with your children. Use the articles in this chapter as an aid. The following questions will help you.

—Do I spend time with my child? How much?

—Do I listen when my child speaks to me?

—Do I give reasons for my decisions?

—Do I ever ignore my child, refuse to answer, or mainly use conversation as a chance to move ahead my own concerns?

—Will my child confide in me?

—Will my child bring problems to me?

ACTIVITY

Hold a Family Meeting to discuss communication. As a conversation starter, parents and children could independently answer the questions listed above under **Taking Stock**. You may find these suggestions answer the useful:

1. Twenty minutes is a good length for such a meeting.
2. Don't be defensive when kids point out your flaws.
3. If you have been wrong, tell the kids you are sorry and that you are going to do better.
4. There may not be much conversation, but don't be frustrated. Building communication takes time, work, and patience.

PLAN FOR ACTION

Improving Family Communication

1. Spending More Time Talking

- Review the past week, asking how much time you spent in conversation with each child. Don't be surprised if your rough estimate adds up to only a few minutes.
- Using the articles in this section, make a list of options that could help increase the time you spend talking with your children.
- Pick the one option that fits best in your family circumstances and start doing it today. Do it again tomorrow. And the next day . . .

2. Eliminating Your Worst Flaw

- Make a list of all the things you do that hurt communication with your children.
- Identify which behavior pattern does the most damage. (If you don't know, your kids can probably tell you what it is.)

- Admit the problem, resolve to change, and decide what steps you must take. Ask the Holy Spirit to help you change.
- Use the articles in this section and resources recommended below for help.

3. If you think your family has such serious communications problems that self-help won't work, set fear and pride aside, and get assistance from a family counselor. Your parish or local Catholic Social Services can refer you.

RESOURCES

Magazine

- *Veritas* **Catholic Youth Magazine,** edited by Paul Lauer. Gives an upbeat, faith-filled Catholic perspective on life for teenagers. Bi-monthly; $14.50 per year. Write for trial subscription; you will receive an invoice for a one-year subscription, which you can cancel if you are not satisfied. For information or subscription, write to Veritas Communications, P.O. Box 8033, Syracuse, NY 13217.

Teenagers

- *How to Get Your Teenager to Talk to You,* edited by Youth for Christ (Victor Books).
- Jim Auer, *10 Good Reasons to Be a Catholic: A Teenager's Guide to the Church* (Liguori).
- Jim Auer, *10 Steps to God: Spirituality for Teens* (Liguori).
- John Bertolucci, *Straight from the Heart: A Call to the New Generation* (Servant).
- Joseph Moore, *When a Teenager Chooses You—as Friend, Confidante, Confirmation Sponsor* (St. Anthony Messenger).

Retreats/Organizations

- *National Evangelization Teams (NET).* NET is a retreat ministry that brings Catholic teenagers into a personal relationship with Jesus Christ. In the last eight years, NET has trained over 450 young Catholic adults to share their faith with hundreds of thousands of Catholic young people in the United States, Canada, and Australia. For information about NET and its availability in your diocese, write to Mark Berchem, Executive Director: NET, 150 N. Smith Avenue, St. Paul, MN 55102.

- *REACH Youth Ministries* mobilizes teams of young adults to share the gospel with Catholic teenagers through a wide variety of retreats, weekends, and programs. REACH is a recognized agency of the Diocese of Yakima, Washington, and serves youth in the Northwest. For information write Tim Briffett, Director: REACH Youth Ministries, 1704 Grant, Yakima, WA 98902.

SEVEN

Rooting Kids in the Catholic Heritage

As Catholic parents our chief tasks include assuring that our children understand the truths of the faith and encouraging our children to believe in them.

Make Friends with the Saints

Our children will see in these heroic men and women the gospel come to life and perhaps be captivated, as the saints were, by the love of God.

Cindy Cavnar

A few years ago my son came to me with a complaint. "Mom," he said, "religion class is boring. Our teacher talks about God and the church but I feel like I've heard it all before." Since he was only nine at the time, I knew he hadn't. After some discussion we got to the point. "The problem is," Matt finally decided, "she doesn't tell any stories about the saints."

His conclusion intrigued me. Thirty years ago a child might easily have had the opposite complaint. Back in that

133

heyday of Catholic devotionalism, the saints were everywhere whether you liked it or not. I happened to like it and, with a little judicious sifting to separate fact from fiction, developed a lifelong affection for these heroic men and women.

Today, as my son discovered at school, the saints have fallen victim to neglect, either ignored or treated with the bemused tolerance usually reserved for an eccentric relative. In the process, we Catholics have lost touch with our history, denying ourselves an acquaintance with an astonishing range of personalities. We've also lost a tremendous source of inspiration, overlooking the very people who can show us what it means to live wholeheartedly for God.

Surely the time has come to rediscover the saints, especially if we intend to root our children in their Catholic heritage. The children themselves will offer no resistance to our efforts to introduce the saints, recognizing a good story when they hear one.

Their response will generally be enthusiastic though we may occasionally harbor doubts as to their true motives, as I recently did with my six-year-old son. Tim announced one day that he wanted to be a saint. Naturally I was pleased and asked him why. "They do neat things and they love the Lord," Tim replied. He paused then added, in a reference to the weightlessness experienced by some saints in prayer, "They also float. That would be fun."

Every parent knows that most activities involving children operate on a fundamental principle: Be honest. You'll never put anything past the kids anyway. This has particular relevance when discussing the saints. Over the years I've discovered that many adults find stories of the saints depressing, irrelevant, or—particularly with some martyrs—gruesome. As one woman told me, "All these people ever seemed to do was suffer." If you have reservations along these lines, take stock of your own attitude before you approach your children.

Sometimes a faulty understanding of the saints when we were young obscures our ability to appreciate them as adults. The primary mistake Catholics make in this area is to focus on what an individual did or how much he suffered rather than on his relationship with the Lord. This emphasis can be frustrating since few of us will ever found a religious

---

Today, the saints have fallen victim to neglect; we Catholics have lost touch with our history, denying ourselves an aquaintance with an astonishing range of personalities.

---

order or preach to the pope. Even fewer of us long for martyrdom. It may help to know that the inordinate attention sometimes paid to a saint's accomplishments or suffering is more a product of shaky theology and overly zealous teachers than of church teaching. If we honor the saints primarily for their love for God, as the church intends, we'll find their example helpful rather than depressing or unattainable.

Developing a Plan for Introducing Your Children to the Saints. To change a less than positive attitude in this area, start by asking the Lord to help you find the truth. At the same time, read some good books about great Catholic men and women, such as *Ten Christians* or *No Strangers to Violence, No Strangers to Love,* both by Fr. Boniface Hanley. One of the most helpful ways you can involve your children with the saints is to name them after one. This ancient practice sets the patron saint before the child as both a model and an intercessor on the child's behalf. If you've already missed this opportunity, however, you can help your child achieve the same purpose through the choice of a confirmation name. The custom of choosing a saint's name to add to one's own at confirmation may seem insignificant, but don't dismiss it lightly. Consider my husband's experience.

Nick gave careful consideration to his confirmation name and chose Matthew in honor of the biblical saint. He admired Matthew particularly for his response when Jesus called him: the tax collector got up, left everything, and followed the Lord.

Unfortunately, a few years after confirmation Nick abandoned his faith, dropped out of school, and began to live in serious sin. He continued this way for several years until one day, on a visit to his family, he attended a prayer meeting where God intervened dramatically in his life. Nick returned to the Lord at that meeting and shortly after went to confession and Mass for the first time in years. The Gospel at Mass that day was the call of Matthew. Nick knew, at that

All About Angels

Sleepy, pink-pajamaed little girls find me no matter what room I pray in before the day begins. Every mother will agree that regardless of what hour you get up, your little ones somehow know about it and find you. Each time they find me, I have to choose to make my greeting one of heartfelt welcome and not irritation. I promised that when the children saw me reading my Bible and praying, their impression of me should not be an angry one: "Uh oh, Mom is praying!"

"Mom, what does this say?" they ask, pointing to the Bible passage I am reading. Again, the choice. Do I hustle them back to their rooms to play, or do I read to them from the Bible? Honestly, I do both.

moment, that this saint had faithfully interceded for him.

Since occasions such as baptism and confirmation are infrequent, parents need to find other ways to interest their children in the saints. One of the most helpful is simply to follow the church's pattern for the saints' feast days, discussing various saints as their days come up. I stay in touch with these occasions by using a calendar that comes with the saint's name printed on the appropriate day for his or her feast. Not all the saints are listed, of course, only two or three major ones per week. (Nor do I talk about all of these. There is such a thing as overkill.) The calendars are available at Catholic bookstores.

Near the calendar I keep the *Pocket Dictionary of Saints* by John J. Delaney (Doubleday). This is a compendium of saints in alphabetical order with a short biography of each. With both the calendar and dictionary at hand, I can easily spot a particular saint and find enough information to give my kids some idea of the identity and life of the individual.

continued on next page

Striking a Balance. I try to balance my "need" to pray and read Scripture with a sensitivity to the Holy Spirit wanting to touch these precious lives he's entrusted to me. The other day I heard the telltale shuffle of feet drawing near. Hug, kiss, snuggle. "What are you reading, Mom?"

"Well, I'm really interested in angels, and I'm trying to find out about them in the Bible." This led to a special time for us that morning. I tried to find stories where angels appeared. Zechariah, Joseph, Mary, and the shepherds at Jesus' birth were visited by messengers of God. An angel rolled back the stone at the tomb of Jesus, and angels appeared to the guards and to the women who sought Jesus.

"Read some more about angels, Mom." Well, I remembered that God also sent angels to the three men in the

continued on next page

Whenever possible, I expand on this approach. Recently, for example, on the feast of John Bosco, I decided to call a little more attention to this cheerful nineteenth-century priest who dedicated his life to children. I took a coffee cake from the freezer and, while it was heating, I quickly picked a few short stories to read from the excellent *Stories from Don Bosco* by Peter Lappin. While the children ate the coffee cake, I read to them from the book and they left for school in good humor, talking about the mysterious dog, Grigio, who miraculously came to John Bosco's rescue whenever his life was threatened by his many enemies.

Someone once said that "words instruct, but good example attracts." That, of course, is part of the timeless appeal of the saints. When Augustine was struggling toward his tumultuous conversion, an account of the life of St. Anthony of the Desert drew him closer to his goal. Ignatius Loyola, recovering from wounds sustained in battle, found himself with nothing to read but a life of Christ and some lives of the saints. So impressed was he that he gave up his

fiery furnace and to Daniel in the lion's den. It seemed that besides being God's version of Federal Express delivering messages in person, they rescued God's people from certain disaster. And that reminded me about guardian angels.

The children's eyes were riveted on me. This was better than a fairy tale. Imagine your own angel! Then I dug out some pictures of angels. I like the strong, tender portraits rather than the Rubenesque, chubby types. I was able to tell them about God's custom-designed plan for their lives, about his personal love for them, and about their having their own guardian angels.

The next morning, while I was thanking the Lord for that special time with them, I heard the familiar shuffling. Oh no! I thought, I'm having a great time praying. Lord, please not again.

wealth and position to serve the Lord.

The saints are as active today as ever. Years ago a friend of mine joined the Hare Krishna sect. After some months, she went home to tell her Catholic family of her decision. They were appalled but Louise remained adamant. Shortly before she was to return to her new life, Louise went to the library to find books related to some research she was doing. She took the elevator to the wrong floor by mistake and found herself in the religious books section near the writings of St. Teresa of Avila. Louise took some of the books home, read them, and was deeply moved by the way Teresa spoke of the Lord. Shortly after, prompted in part by Teresa's writings, she returned to the church.

We can take them or leave them, but the saints will always be there for us and for our children. Let's not deny our kids their friendship and intercession. They will see in these heroic men and women the gospel come to life and perhaps be captivated—as the saints were—by the love of God. ■

"Mom, what does your Bible say today? More angels?" So there we were snuggled on the couch, reading about Jesus healing the blind man. Their spirits were so touched that morning, that later in the car pool returning from school, they said, "Mom, tell Laura all about those angels and blind people in the Bible."

I recalled how after his resurrection Jesus had talked with the two men on the road to Emmaus. They did not recognize him until he broke bread with them. "Were not our hearts burning within us," they said, "while he spoke to us on the way and opened the scriptures to us?" (See Luke 24: 32.)

I realized that when I break the Word of God with my girls their hearts burn within them as they meet Jesus in Scripture.

Therese Cirner

Developing a New Catholic Body Language

*Tips for expressing our Catholic heritage
in everyday family life.*

Therese Boucher

At one time it was easy to tell which kids were Catholic. They brought tuna or egg sandwiches to school on Fridays, and had their foreheads smeared with ashes one Wednesday in late winter. One priest described it as a religion of smells and bells and foreign sounds. All very mystifying and appealing to the senses, all very recognizable.

What makes our children Catholic now? The practices that distinguished us as Catholics when we were growing up have been put on the shelf, or they have been transformed. Novenas, for example, now appear in parish bulletins as "evenings of renewal." Since Vatican II, attention has shifted from external practices to interior life. If you and your family are experiencing a vital relationship with Jesus, Father-God, and Holy Spirit, there is Good News to live by. As we give our hearts to the Lord Jesus, the Gospel readings and even the prayers of the Sunday liturgy have new clarity. We become more Catholic from the roots up, as it were. Liturgy gets worked into daily life. One family I know, for example, asks each member to listen to the readings for a favorite or puzzling sentence. Then they share what they heard on the way home in the car.

This transformation is like putting a plant into a new pot. Along with growth, there can also be the danger of shock to roots and plant for a time. Not to worry. If this has happened to you, you have millions of Catholics to struggle along with. We are faced with the challenge of developing a new Catholic "body language," a way to recognize each other and share faith in Jesus as part of a very diverse church community.

A big part of this adjustment is our desire to nurture our children as Catholic Christians. And when we notice things our parental responsibility prompts us to do, we may shrink back at the challenge.

Let's look at our Catholic heritage for clues as to how to integrate our daily lives and the life of Jesus in the church. The questions: Who? What? Where? and When? can help us in our quest.

The What. What we want to share is based in our understanding of what the church is. Avery Dulles says there are at least five models we cling to: herald of God's Word, servant of human needs, sacrament of God's presence, supportive community, and structured institution. We should combine several of these in our own personal picture of the church in order to have a balanced perspective. I suggest that parents read *Becoming a Catholic Even if You Happen to Be One* by James J. Killgallon (Chicago: ACTA Foundation: 1980) for help in sorting out what the church is for you. Emily Dickinson expresses my own favorite model: "Love is the fellow of the Resurrection scooping up the dust and chanting 'Live!' "

The church is a touch-and-see, sacramental reality. To act this out, I like to bring my children into the church building alone and give them a tour of the objects we use to worship. I once did this with a little boy who was unchurched, just a curious passerby. I explained and even let him touch. As he left, he said, "Nice place you have here!"

The Who. To foster a community model of church for our children, it is important that we bring them to parish events and develop relationships with those around us on Sunday. This is one way to show them who the Catholic church is. Each week, for example, you might introduce your family to someone you see. You might teach the children to leave extra room at the end of the pew for strangers.

The Who of our Catholic faith has other dimensions, too. We share membership with millions of believers who have lived before us through thousands of years, and with generations to come after us. In the 1950s Bishop Fulton Sheen had a weekly television show teaching a whole generation about God. When he won an Emmy for his work, he publicly thanked his writers: Matthew, Mark, Luke, and John. It is this connectedness we want to convey to our children.

The When. Our faith invites us to be sensitive to our history and our future as church. A simple trip to a museum can show us the faith of centuries depicted by so many artists, sculptors, and painters. The American Catholic past has also made its mark on us. For example, the Baltimore Catechism, a document that came from the Council of Baltimore in 1884, introduced many of us to the faith. More recently we have experienced the reforms of the Second Vatican Council, including the renewal of the liturgy, as well as a nudge to experience mature faith through its findings. How much do we know about these important documents?

You may find it helpful to study some church history yourself. Consult such popularly written books as Alan Schreck's *Compact History of the Catholic Church* (Servant) and F. Michael Perko's *Catholic and American* (Our Sunday Visitor).

The Where. Finally, our faith means we need to take an honest look at parish and family practices. Are we committed to a parish? Are we able to communicate our needs while being sensitive to how difficult it is to sort through those of the whole parish? Do we support good liturgies and parish programs? Do we encourage our deacons, catechists, pastors, lectors, and others directly involved in parish work?

Do we make our homes places of faith through use of objects such as Bibles, crucifixes, a prayer corner, and religious music? We may want to join those families who spend time watching Catholic television such as Mother Angelica's Eternal Word Television Network. We can take as models those who enliven their faith by praying at meals and by adopting cultural celebrations for holy days, like Christmas. For example, we can imitate French and Spanish cultures that use a procession to put the baby Jesus in the manger on Christmas.

Our goal as parents today should be to integrate our faith and our life. As we share the *Who, What, Why,* and *Where* of our faith, our children will grow along with us. Parents are the primary religious educators. First, by example; then, in the kind of classes we choose for our children. Some parents choose simple projects to do at home with one or more children to supplement what is offered in the parish. *In My Heart Room: Sixteen Love Prayers for Little Children* by Mary Terese Donze, A.S.C. (Liguori) offers simple Christian meditation exercises. *Storytelling—It's Easy* by Ethel Barrett (Zondervan) can help you sharpen storytelling skills for bedtime use. Finally, my book, *Becoming a Sensuous Catechist* (Twenty-Third Publications) offers activities for all age levels.

An Example Drawn from Our Family Life. Early one Lent we went on a pilgrimage to the Weston Priory in Vermont. We took a prayer walk in the woods and collected a small fallen branch to make a crucifix. At home we rolled newspaper tubes and fashioned Jesus' body by joining two lengths with masking tape. Features were added with magic markers. Later on Good Friday we gathered around our homemade crucifix for a prayer service, using the Gospel story and the song "Lift High the Cross."

There are countless ways of passing on our heritage as Catholic parents. Find the ones you enjoy and can be most comfortable with. All the conscious and unconscious efforts we make become a kind of body language. After all, we *are* the church, our children's first answer to "Who is Jesus to us?" and "What makes us Catholic?" ■

Why We Send Our Children to a Catholic School

While Catholic schools cannot replace parents as the primary religious educator, they can show our children that they belong to a community whose love is at work in the world outside our homes.

Mitch Finley

One hears many arguments for and against sending children to Catholic schools. We have Catholic friends who grow nearly livid as they insist that Catholic schools are outmoded and a waste of human and financial resources. Others say that they do not think that sending their children to a Catholic school would be worth the expense. "In some parts of the country I could see sending our kids to a Catholic school," remarked one friend. "But here the public schools are just as good as the Catholic schools, so why spend all that money?" Another friend claims that Catholic schools insulate kids from the real world, and it is unfair to do that. I respond that it all depends on what he means by "real."

I would like to explain the bottom-line reason my wife, Kathy, and I want our children to attend Catholic schools—why we're willing to embrace whatever sacrifices it takes to see that they do.

We want our boys to receive a good education. We want them to have dedicated and well-trained teachers and the opportunity to develop academically to their potential. Our basic motive for sending them to a Catholic school is, however, a religious one.

We do not believe that a Catholic school can or should accept responsibility for our children's religious formation. Parents who, consciously or unconsciously, hand over their children to a Catholic school with this goal in mind may well be in for a deep disappointment. On the contrary, we believe that religious formation happens primarily within the family circle. With few exceptions, parents, not teachers, are the primary religious influence in their children's lives, for good or for ill. All teachers can hope to do is lend a helping hand.

We do, however, expect a Catholic school to perform an invaluable task—to give a wider dimension to our children's understanding of Christian faith. We want our children to learn from experience that religion has to do with all of life. It is not meant to be unpacked only at certain times and is not only a private and family matter.

The Main Reason Why. By sending our children to a Catholic school, we hope to give them a chance to learn that the Christian faith is meant to be one with the fabric of their everyday lives. "See," we are saying to our kids, "even at school it's OK to bring up God and Jesus and other religious topics." And school is a large part, indeed, of a child's world.

Though it is not structured explicitly into times spent on geography and math, a Catholic school's message to students is that God is present in such "nonreligious" studies, too. God is as much a part of playground relationships as God is present when we join hands to pray around our family table. It's OK to draw pictures of Jesus and Mary and talk about them, in school as well as at home. It's good to learn to pray with one's classmates and teacher because the sacred is in the ordinary.

We cherish our U.S. citizenship, but we believe that the dominant culture sometimes conflicts with a Christian lifestyle and spirituality. We want our children to understand that there are alternatives, and that it's good not to go along simply in order to get along. Respect other people's rights, but stick to the truth. Be willing to stick your neck out for others, to hold your own if the occasion calls for it.

We want our children to learn from experience that religion has to do with all of life. It is not meant to be unpacked only at certain times and is not only a private and family matter.

The Catholic school our children attend supports the values and perspectives we try to pass along to them at home. As parents we crave more support, not more competition.

To put it another way, we applaud words from the U.S. bishops' 1972 pastoral letter, *To Teach as Jesus Did*: "Since the Christian vocation is a call to transform oneself and society with God's help, the educational efforts of the church must encompass the twin purposes of personal sanctification and social reform in light of Christian values."

A Christian community is challenged by the gospel to live in and for, but not of, the world. If Catholic schools today sometimes have a problem, it is with the temptation to overlook the gap that always exists between a gospel perspective and the dominant culture. We object to Catholic schools that try to blend in with the "establishment" to the point that they lose this faith-inspired, countercultural spirit. We object when Catholic school administrators worry about whether a course on social justice will offend the local business community or the wealthy parents of certain students.

Kathy and I each spent several years in Catholic grade schools in the 1950s, and we both graduated from Catholic high schools (and later Catholic colleges and graduate schools). We can tell our share of Catholic-school stories, but more powerful than the very real limitations we encountered in the Catholic schools of yesterday is the conviction that there was something special about those years.

What was it? When we try to pin down reasons for our long-lasting positive feelings about Catholic schools all we can think of is the sense of belonging (we call it "community" today)—the feeling that we were cared for and the constant, gentle determination to share with us, the students, a quiet and dependable mystery at the center of which was love. We find this spirit still in our children's Catholic school. The teachers are good, and these days the halls are painted with brightly colored rainbows and butterflies. But those are incidentals, and the mystery is still there, quiet and warm.

This is our hope: that our children, too, will gain from attending a Catholic school a lasting experience of the gentle, reliable, mysterious love at work in the wider world outside our home. That is not something kids are likely to find in a public school, no matter how good that school is in other ways. Thus, we believe that what Catholic school children get is a more complete education.

For us, this is reason enough to send our children to a Catholic school. ■

Think, Pray, & Act

UNDERSTANDING OUR CATHOLIC ROOTS

FOR REFLECTION AND DISCUSSION

1. How can we communicate our faith and values to our kids? (See articles by Boucher and Cirner.)
2. Why should we talk to our kids about Catholic history? (See article by Boucher.)
3. What can appreciation of the saints do for our children? (See article by Cavnar.)
4. What are some reasons for considering sending children to Catholic schools? (See article by Finley.)

TAKING STOCK

1. *How Well Do I Understand Catholicism?* Take a bead on how well you know your faith by responding to the following questions:
   a. Can I explain in my own words the meaning of the following doctrines:
      —the incarnation;
      —the resurrection;
      —the ascension;
      —the apostolic succession;
      —the immaculate conception.
   b. Can I answer the following questions commonly asked of Catholics?
      • Why do Catholics pray for the dead?
      • Do Catholics really worship Mary?

- What do Catholics believe happens to people when they die?
- What do Catholics believe about the Bible?
- What is the meaning of the Mass?
- Why do Catholics have sacraments?

c. Can I answer the following questions about the church?
- Where did the church come from?
- Why do we have a pope and bishops?
- What was Vatican II?
- Why do we have parishes?
- What does papal infallibility mean?

d. If this exercise persuades you that you have a lot to learn, go on to the **Plan For Action.**

PLAN FOR ACTION

If we are going to introduce our kids to the Catholic heritage, we have to expand our own understanding of the faith. You don't need to know it all up front in order to begin teaching your children. However, you must study and learn *yourself* as you raise your kids Catholic.

Here are some suggestions about how to get started studying your faith:

- Identify the areas you are least informed about and list questions to which you don't know the answer.
- Consult the books and magazines listed under **Resources** at the end of every chapter to get more information and answers.
- Read an article or a book in the area you feel least informed about.
- Keep up with the life of the church by regularly reading your diocesan newspaper and a Catholic periodical.

(See the list of Catholic magazines in **Resources** for chapter four.)

- Take advantage of your parish's adult education program and the parish library if there is one.

ACTIVITY

For Children Ten and Under: Take the kids to visit a local Catholic church at a time when no services are going on. Be sure to call attention to the baptistry, where babies and others are introduced into the life of Christ and the church; the pulpit, from which we hear the Word of God; the altar, around which we gather to worship at Mass; the confessional, where we can get reconciled with God; the tabernacle, where Jesus is present in a special way. Let them bless themselves with holy water, to remind them of their baptism. Show and explain to them statues, stained glass windows, the stations of the cross, candles, hymnals, kneelers, sacred vessels and vestments—if they are in sight—and anything else that gets their attention. To get ready for the visit, you may have to study up on some of these things yourself.

For Families with Children over Ten: Select a well-told life of a saint and have it read aloud to the family. For help and ideas, refer to Cindy Cavnar's article and to **Resources** (below). Let the children ask questions and try to find the answers in the story. Ask questions about important points: Why did St. Francis leave his family's wealth? Why did St. Maximilian Kolbe offer to die in the place of another man in a Nazi concentration camp? Why does Mother Teresa show affection to AIDS patients? And so on.

RESOURCES

Catholic Faith

(See also **Resources** for chapters one, three, and five.)

- Felician A. Foy and Rose M. Avato, *A Concise Guide to the Catholic Church: History, Saints, Feasts, Glossary* (Our Sunday Visitor).
- James J. Killgallon, *Becoming a Catholic Even if You Happen to Be One* (ACTA Foundation).
- Alan Schreck with Wendy Leifeld, *Your Catholic Faith: A Question-and-Answer Catechism* (Servant).
- Francis A. Sullivan, S.J., *The Church We Believe In: One, Holy, Catholic, Apostolic* (Paulist Press).

Saints and Storytelling

- Ethel Barrett, *Storytelling—It's Easy* (Zondervan).
- William J. Bausch, *Storytelling: Imagination and Faith* (Twenty-Third Publications).
- Robert Charlebois, and others, *Saints for Kids by Kids*, (Liguori).
- John J. Delaney, editor, *Pocket Dictionary of Saints* (Doubleday).
- Charles Dollen, editor, *Prayer Book of the Saints* (Our Sunday Visitor).
- Boniface Hanley, O.F.M., *No Strangers to Violence, No Strangers to Love* (Ave Maria Press).
- Boniface Hanley, O.F.M., *Ten Saints* (Ave Maria Press).
- Victor Hoagland, C.P., *The Book of Saints: The Lives of the Saints According to the Liturgical Calendar* (Regina Press).
- Albert J. Nevins, *A Saint for Your Name* (Saints for Boys) and *A Saint for Your Name* (Saints for Girls) (Our Sunday Visitor).

Church History

(See also **Resources** for chapter one.)

- William J. Bausch, *Pilgrim Church: A Popular History of Catholic Christianity* (Twenty-Third Publications).
- Edward Day, C.S.S.R., *The Catholic Church Story: Changing and Changeless* (Liguori).
- F. Michael Perko, *Catholic and American* (Our Sunday Visitor).
- Alan Schreck, *Compact History of the Catholic Church* (Servant).

Family Prayer and Celebrations

(See also **Resources** for chapters four and five.)

- Therese Boucher, *Becoming a Sensuous Catechist* (Twenty-Third Publications).
- Sandra DeGidio, *Enriching Faith Through Family Celebrations* (Twenty-Third Publications).
- Evelyn Birge Vitz, *A Continual Feast: A Cookbook to Celebrate the Joys of Family and Faith Throughout the Christian Year* (Harper & Row).

EIGHT

Training Kids in Catholic Morality

Parents must show and tell their kids how God wants them to deal with sin in their own lives and in society.

Helping Kids Deal with Sin

When children are suffering from a dose of healthy guilt, discipline can teach them a cosmic lesson.

John C. Blattner

Every parent knows "The Look." You come home from the grocery store and find the remains of a shattered jar scattered across the kitchen floor: shards of glass lying in pools of dill pickle juice. You go into the bathroom and find a pile of towels that have been used to dry off the family basketball court (that is, the driveway) after a spring rain. You try to open the door to the basement and find it tied shut with several yards of mint-flavored, unwaxed dental floss.

You have a pretty good idea who the culprit is. (Just because you weren't there to witness the crime doesn't mean you can't recognize your seven-year-old's *modus operandi*.) But when you confront him with the evidence all you get is . . . "The Look." The wide eyes gazing up at you oh-so-innocently the mouth slightly agape in wounded astonishment.

Who, me? Nope. Never seen it before. Haven't reached for a pickle in weeks. Don't you believe me?

You don't.

And now you have a real problem. Dropping a pickle jar is one thing. An accident. Could happen to anyone.

But dropping a pickle jar and then claiming innocence: that's more serious. That's lying. That's sin. Now what do you do?

Let's start with what you don't do.

You don't just roll your eyes, shake your head, and walk away muttering under your breath. Nor do you slide into your Mt. Vesuvius impression and blow your cool all over the walls. No, you rejoice.

Rejoice?

That's right. Rejoice. You have found yourself smack in the middle of a golden opportunity to score a point for the kingdom of God. An opportunity to teach your child an important spiritual lesson: about the reality of sin, the inevitability of judgment, and the opportunity for reconciliation.

The Reality of Sin. You may have noticed how much difficulty children have picking up words like "yes" and "share," and the relative ease with which they master "no!" and "mine!" You could swear sometimes that your precious little ones are born with a predisposition to do wrong.

Well, you're right. Kids—even our kids, yours and mine— are born with a predisposition to do wrong. It's called original sin, and recognizing it takes a lot of the mystery out of raising children.

Sin is not a very popular topic these days. But it is a fact nevertheless. Trying to pretend it doesn't exist, either in ourselves or in our kids, is like trying to pretend the law of gravity doesn't exist.

And it's confusing to kids as well. Now, some people say children are born in a state of blissful innocence, and only develop hang-ups about concepts like sin later, when well-intentioned but misguided grown-ups (like parents or priests) lay guilt trips on them.

I think it works just the other way around. We're born with an innate sense that some things are right to do and other things are wrong, and with a faculty for feeling guilt when we've done wrong. I mean healthy guilt: the kind that alerts us to moral danger the way our physical senses alert us to physical danger.

Even kids have this faculty. They don't quite understand it, and they don't know what to call it (conscience, in case you've forgotten), but they know it's there. And their little world makes more sense when we help them understand it, and teach them what to call it. It's the well-intentioned grown-ups who tell them to disregard this inborn spiritual sensing device, and who teach them that there is no such thing as sin, who are really the misguided ones.

The Inevitability of Judgment. When I was a teenager, I went one day to a local shopping mall with a friend of mine. He swiped a record album, slipping it into a shopping bag, and I was his accomplice.

"We'd better get out of here," I hissed, as I had noticed a suspicious-looking adult start moving purposefully in our direction. But it was too late. We both got hauled into the store's security office for shoplifting.

It was a long ride home, as I recall. I can still feel the burning sensation in my cheeks. The shame of it!

My parents were angry, of course. But, curiously, they

were also glad. Not that I had done wrong, but that I had been caught in the attempt. Maybe it would teach me a lesson.

It did. Now that I am a parent, I know just how they felt. I hope my kids get caught the first time, too. It'll help dispel the tragically wrong-headed notion that sin goes unpunished.

In this world, of course, sin often does go unpunished. But we need to teach our children that there is more to life than what happens in this world, that there is a heaven above us and a hell beneath us and a God who really does settle accounts with awesome justice at the end.

We do our kids no favor when we wink at sin and withhold deserved punishment. In fact, to do so is to tell a cosmic lie, to fundamentally mislead our children about the nature of reality.

The Opportunity for Reconciliation. Now we come to the indispensable third part of the lesson, and the uniquely Christian part: that God offers us the opportunity to be reconciled to him despite our sin. Sin and judgment are facts of life for everyone. But reconciliation comes only for those who are in Christ Jesus. Because of what he did for us, we can be restored to fellowship with God despite both our sinfulness and our sins. We can be forgiven. We can be reconciled.

This is the context, I think, in which to bring up spanking. Surprised? To most of us, spanking is a thoroughly negative thing. We associate it exclusively with pain, anger, and rejection.

But I don't see it that way. I've learned to associate spanking (indeed, all discipline) with joy and love and reconciliation.

Now, I won't try to deny that a little anger sometimes creeps in around the edges. And certainly pain is of the essence of spanking (think of it as a sort of emphatic non-verbal communication).

But rejection? No way. I don't discipline my kids despite my love for them. I discipline them because I love them. The Bible says as much: "He who spares his rod hates his son, but he who loves him takes care to chastise him" (Prv 13:24).

Note the word "careful." Our discipline is to be "full of care." Our motive must always be to teach and to restore, never to hurt or destroy.

There is an art to giving a good spanking. It starts in an atmosphere of peace. If you're hot and bothered, wait until the anger passes. Take the time to explain what's going on: what the child did, why it was wrong, why it deserves punishment. Make sure the spanking stings, but also make sure it does no damage. Afterwards, take lots of time for hugs and kisses and loving words. I made it a policy years ago never to leave the scene of a spanking until both my child and I are smiling and able to say, "I love you," and mean it.

In addition to spanking, many parents use other forms of discipline, especially for older children. These include such dreadful punishments as grounding and removal of telephone or driving privileges. Administered with care and affection, these can also effectively teach our kids how to handle their sin and guilt and be opportunities for reconciliation with God and with us.

Reconciliation can include other elements, too. Apologizing to those we've hurt and "making it up" to them when possible. Undoing the negative effects of our actions (cutting the dental floss off the doorknob, for instance). Memorizing passages of Scripture that underscore healthy attitudes and righteous actions. And, of course, receiving the sacrament of reconciliation when the child is old enough and the offense is serious enough.

I wouldn't say my kids exactly enjoy discipline. But they

do understand it. They never doubt for a moment that I love them, and that acceptance and love are waiting on the other side of momentary pain. The Bible says about God that "his anger lasts but a moment; a lifetime, his good will" (Ps 30:6).

Wouldn't you rejoice if your kids could learn that facet of God's nature through what they've experienced from you? ■

Morality Begins at Home

Early lessons learned in the family shape a child's behavior for life. Here are four rules to help parents teach their kids how to make moral choices.

Ralph F. Ranieri

A young couple with three children no longer attended church. Consequently they were not bringing their children up in the church. Yet this couple had been taught the fundamentals of religion by church-going parents. The man had even attended a Christian college for two years.

"I don't take my children to church," he said, "because of the guilt. I had such a horrible sense of guilt instilled in me by the church. I don't want my kids to experience the same thing."

Guilt is terrible when it gets out of control. People will do almost anything to avoid it. Like this couple, some will stop going to church if they see that as the cause of their guilt. But in a more subtle way, others will refrain from teaching their children moral principles in order to avoid guilt. Still others will teach moral principles, but they will do it in a half-hearted way. These people think that if they don't show too much conviction their kids will learn the moral principles without the guilt.

From my years as a counselor, I know just how much pain unnecessary guilt can cause. But there is only one thing worse than growing up with too much guilt, and that's growing up with no guilt at all.

A friend of mine jokes that he doesn't worry about his children growing up with guilt. "A good therapist can straighten out someone with too much guilt," he goes on to say, "but there's little hope for a person who has no sense of guilt."

People with no sense of guilt are the scourge of society. They don't know where their rights end and someone else's begin. They feel no social responsibility. In short, we can't trust them because they don't play by the rules.

In order to teach your children right from wrong and help them become caring members of society, you must run the risk of giving them some guilt. And this is perfectly acceptable. We all need just the right amount of guilt to make us responsible. We need to feel a twinge of conscience now and then. If we are to be truly moral, we must learn to think twice about an action. It takes a certain amount of courage to teach your children morality. You'll need to trust your own judgment, your child's tolerance, and God's grace. If you teach with humility, you will not have to worry. People who err in teaching morals are usually those who take extreme positions, thinking that they have nothing to teach or that they are absolutely right and should be followed to the letter.

But if you are humble parents and rely on the grace of God, the moral lessons your children learn from you will be the most important lessons they learn in life.

First, they are important lessons because children learn them early in life; they help lay the very foundation of their personalities. Second, the lessons taught at home are important because they are learned over and over again and are frequently reinforced. This gives the child a chance to turn a good lesson into a good habit.

Rule 1: The First Rule for Teaching Morality to Your Children, Regardless of Their Age, Is to Use Your Own Example. I know that you have heard it a hundred times, but it is still paramount. Nothing teaches like example.

Sometimes the influence of a parent's example on a child is just so obvious. So many children are angry because their parents are angry. So many children show prejudice because their parents show prejudice. So many children aren't interested in reading because their parents don't read.

Most parents have trouble getting their children to do yard work. But I knew a man who loved to do yard work. It wasn't coincidental that he often had to talk his children out of doing the work, so that he could do it.

Our children's antennae are always out, picking up feelings, attitudes, values, and priorities which they often unconsciously assimilate into their own personalities. Therefore the value of example as a teaching tool cannot be overemphasized.

But what does this mean? Do parents have to be saints to teach morality? Of course not. If that were the case, we'd never be able to teach morality in the home.

All you have to do to teach morality by example is to be humble, honest, and sincere. Try. Admit your failings. And try again. Duplicity confuses children, not honest mistakes.

Experts say that abusive parents were usually abused as children, and that the drinking patterns of parents affect the way teens handle alcohol. But a big part of the effect—although I've never seen any studies on it—has to do with the honesty of the parent. Children often fail to learn the correct moral response because their parents are saying one thing and doing the other.

Children would get a completely different picture if the

parent said, "I'm too angry with you, son. I need help to act patiently." Or might not the child get a totally different perspective on drinking if Dad said, "Look, I know I drank too much last night. I was wrong, and I'm getting some help so I don't destroy myself"?

Admitting faults and expressing a definite attempt to change doesn't make your faults any less harmful, but it teaches the child that these things are so wrong that you are taking steps to resolve them. The parent who errs and admits it teaches morality by example, too.

We can do this in little ways. One father apologized for using a four-letter-word. A mother told her children she was wrong for saying unkind things about her friends. After grace one evening, a family prayed for all the good that they left undone or for anyone they may have hurt.

So it doesn't take a saint to teach morality by example. It just takes people with a commitment to living Christian lives who refuse to quit or to deny their faults.

Rule 2: Teach Morality at Home in a Normal, Natural, and On-going Manner. Moral lessons shouldn't be reserved for those special moments when Dad sits down with Junior, or Mom sits down with Suzie, to explain once for all the mysteries of life. Morality pertains to more than sex and drugs. It has to do with the way we live and the way we treat one another.

Children do not make moral decisions once a month or even once a week. They make numerous moral decisions every day. In one day Jane, a teenager, made decisions about the following: whether or not to cheat on her homework; whether to go along with her group and tease another student; whether to join friends who were skipping a class; whether to share a beer with a friend; whether to leave a basketball game early and go out to the parking lot with a boy.

Even younger children are constantly making moral

decisions. What to do with their anger, whether to obey, tell the truth, play fair, brag, or tease are all moral decisions. They all have to do with right and wrong and with the way we treat other people.

Because moral questions arise constantly, morality must be taught everyday, wherever you find yourselves—in the car, in the yard, at the dinner table, or in front of the TV. We must be ready to do moral teaching anywhere else the question of right or wrong comes up.

You don't want to make your children feel that every action is a choice between good and evil, sin and virtue. Making children too self-conscious may only cause scruples. What you want to teach is a natural, obvious Christian moral code which governs the way they live. If you are alert to opportunities, you can accomplish a great deal without even appearing to be teaching.

The Time to Teach Morality

There will no doubt be times when Mom or Dad have to "lay down the law" or give the proverbial lecture. But very often the best moral lessons are subtle. They are often spontaneous, and sometimes they are no longer than one sentence. In his goodness God has given us about eighteen years to teach moral lessons to our children. That's not too long, but it is long enough for us to relax. We don't have to teach our children everything in one day. We have time to teach morality over and over in different ways and at different times.

Ralph F. Ranieri

One father found that the TV evening news was one of the best helps for spontaneously teaching morality. "Last night there were a group of angry people on the news shouting racial slurs," the father said. "This gave my son and I a few minutes to discuss hatred and social justice."

Almost every news item contains a moral issue. A story about the dumping of toxic waste is a chance to talk about social responsibility to one another. AIDS, which is constantly in the news, can provide a perfect opportunity to talk about sexual morality without having to make the conversation unbearably formal. Commercials, usually considered as interruptions, can be occasions to talk about materialism. Even though TV may have many drawbacks, you might as well use it to your advantage when you can. Children viewing a program are already attentive, and we can distract them for a moment to speak about a moral question.

There are other opportunities for teaching morality naturally. A mother was saying that her family discusses moral issues all the time, often without even realizing it. At the dinner table her family usually talks about the events of the day. "Inevitably," she says, "someone will talk about a person who hurt them, a friend who asked them to do something 'sneaky,' or just the questionable behavior of people close to them.

"All this," the mother concludes, "gives us a chance to talk about how to handle situations and people."

Rule 3: Relate All Your Moral Teaching to Love. Love is the guiding principle for Christians. Love is the greatest law and all the other laws hinge on it.

You should teach a child not to lie, steal, or ridicule by explaining that such actions violate the law of love. Love is something anyone regardless of age can identify with and make sense of. A prohibition for the sake of a prohibition is harder to understand.

"What's wrong with watching this movie?" a ten-year-old complained as his mother switched the channel. "There is too much killing in it," the mother answered. "Jesus taught us to love and respect one another, not to act like that." The answer made sense to the child, even though he was disappointed about missing the end of his show.

Older children often look for the reason behind a command, and what better reason can there be for either doing or not doing something than the law of love? Love also helps us justify some of the finer points of morality when we're instructing teens.

One father found that teaching his son about sexual responsibility didn't really make sense unless he taught him about love and respect for his own body and that of others. Being sexually responsible takes a certain amount of discipline, but love provides a solid motivation.

When the youth group was dividing up some chores in the parish and going out to homes helping people who needed assistance, Diane planned on skipping the activity. "Sometimes moral choices mean doing something," Diane's mother said. "If you are going to be part of the Christian community, you have to show your love."

Love will help us remember that sometimes morality requires that we reach out. The Gospel example of the Good Samaritan and Jesus' admonitions to feed the hungry, clothe the naked, and visit the imprisoned are calls to moral action, not just bonus activities for those who have done everything else.

Rule 4: Finally, Expect Virtuous Action, but Teach What to Do in Case of Failure. We all expect to reach our destinations safely when we board a plane. Yet the first thing the flight attendants show us is what to do in the event of a disaster. It's good to know just in case.

Since no one is perfect, you must teach your children about God's love and forgiveness. They have to know that they can always start over, no matter what they do. If they grasp this, they will not only continue to love themselves, but they will also be able to love those around them who have sinned.

The most important lessons in life are learned in the home. Lessons learned early in the family are tucked deep in our personalities. They will remain there for a lifetime, prompting and motivating us. Teaching these lessons is not an easy task for any parent. We all need the help of the Holy Spirit to begin teaching morality at home. ■

Talking with Teens about Sex

If parents wait to talk to their kids about sex, someone else, very likely with very different moral values, will do the talking for them.

Connie Marshner

A guest on the "700 Club," I talked about sex education and what parents should do about it. Then I took telephone calls from viewers. One distressed mother relayed a scenario all too common: Her fourteen-year-old Christian daughter had gone to a party, had a few beers, and ended up having intercourse.

I don't remember many more details of her story, but I clearly remember the tone of the woman's voice. She was confused and amazed as to how this could have happened to *her* daughter.

She is not alone in her distress. Author and speaker Josh

McDowell recently released results of a shocking survey. When he polled church-going Christian young people about their sexual principles and practices he found that 43 percent had engaged in intercourse by age eighteen. By age thirteen, 20 percent had engaged in sexual "petting" or in intercourse. And yet 82 percent of these young people claimed to be sincere Christians who knew Christ.

How has it come to this? That's the question every Christian parent should ask. After all, the Bible clearly forbids sexual relations with anyone other than a spouse. A multitude of factors contribute to this plague, specifically these: the pervasive influence of the secular culture, the near absence of straightforward teaching against immorality, and laxity at home.

Proper authority and submission to authority simply do not exist in most teenagers' lives. Even the so-called "family" TV shows portray parents as objects of ridicule and kids as rightfully in control of their own lives.

An attitude of scorn for anyone who isn't "cool," part of the in-crowd, prevails. This gives the peer group a slave-master power—and don't think the pressures to conform to the popular culture vanish when a child crosses the threshold of a parochial school. Even the apostle Paul knew how persuasive peer influence can be. In 1 Corinthians 5:11 he forbade early Christians to keep company with fornicators.

In recent years, what have we been teaching about sexual morality? Frankly, not much. In McDowell's survey, 36 percent of the respondents were not able to state that premarital intercourse was unacceptable behavior. They didn't realize it was wrong, probably because no one had taught them—not the church, not their parents.

The Excuses. Parents give many excuses for not talking to their children about sex and morality. They see the subject as so personal that embarrassment ties their tongue. They have trouble in their own sexual lives, which heightens the frustration. They have tainted pasts and therefore feel hypocritical telling their children to refrain from activity in which they engaged.

The worst excuse: expecting the school to do the job for them. Why would a parent want someone else to teach his or her child about something as important as sexuality? That someone else will likely teach different values from the parent's.

Some parents will expect the church to do the teaching. Though the church should reinforce principles, parents must not forget they have the primary responsibility for all the education of their children—including sex education.

Parents also put off having *the* talk. A while ago I told a Christian mother that I was writing a book about teaching one's children about the sacredness of sex. "Oh, good," she replied. "I'll need that in a few years for my son."

"How old is he?" I asked.

He was nine, and she was sure he knew nothing at all about sex. As our conversation progressed, I simply could not persuade the woman that she couldn't afford to wait "a few years." If that boy attends school, if he plays with other boys, if he watches TV, he is hearing about sex. More important, he is forming his values about it. Even at that age he's more than likely hearing, "Sex is for fun," or, "Girls are made to give boys pleasure."

A young person who has never heard otherwise from a parent will assume that what he's hearing is correct. Children tend to accept what they hear unless they have already absorbed other information on the subject.

I conducted an informal survey last year. Every person who admitted having premarital sex also told me that when he or she was growing up the subject of sex was never mentioned by parents. On the other hand, most of the people who had married as virgins could remember conversations with their parents that had helped them stay on the path of virtue. Scientific surveys indicate similar patterns.

A study commissioned by the Office of Adolescent Pregnancy Programs (U.S. Department of Health and Human Services) identified several factors that correlated with teenage virtue: regular church attendance, a belief that premarital intercourse is "usually or always wrong," academic achievement, and a high level of parental involvement in the teen's life.

Our Responsibility and the Opportunities. If parents wait for a child to ask about sex, a conversation may never take place. A parent has a responsibility to find out where a child is at and what needs he or she has. With a young child, you might use a cat with kittens or a trip to the zoo to start a fact-finding conversation that will help you determine how much your child knows about the making of babies.

Children's questions that aren't directly related to human sexuality can be great opportunities for parents to lay a firm foundation for *the* big talk. A question such as "Do mommy cats and daddy cats love each other very much?" is an open door to a lesson about the uniqueness of human relationships and the sacredness of fatherhood and motherhood in marriage. Two weeks later the child may not remember what you said, but that child will have absorbed an attitude that will help him or her counter the message heard from the media or from friends.

Sooner than may be wished, the day for *the* talk about the proper role of sex will arrive. Relax. Self-disclosure is neither necessary nor desirable. In this role the parent becomes a conveyor of information about: what God expects, the emotional and spiritual consequences of breaking his laws, and the risks of disease and even death that one takes if one does not practice self-control.

Planned Parenthood apparently believes the solution to the teenage pregnancy crisis is sex-control. The organization doesn't expect much from today's teens. Kids will be promiscuous anyhow, they argue, so let's give out contraceptives. But that's not the answer for our children. We need to teach them how to say no.

Again, that message hits the current culture head on. We laugh at a fat feline in the cartoons gobbling up a tray of someone else's lasagna and chocolate cake and then sheepishly explaining, "I couldn't help myself."

Of course the real issue is that he didn't want to "help" himself. Right then, filling that self-centered appetite was simply more important to him than anything else. There's an important prerequisite to self-control—motivation.

Where does a child learn the value of self-control? At home, and by being loved. Real love models self-control. If a child sees a self-indulgent parent, why should he or she act any differently? By a parent's example, a child learns to care for another person, to put someone else's needs ahead of personal desire. Without concern for someone else or for some spiritual cause, there's rarely motivation for someone to deny the flesh.

God provides an instrument to encourage self-control: fasting. As I see it, God wants Christians to fast not because it helps him, but because it helps us. It teaches us to deny the flesh, to say no to that cupcake or steak. As parents fast, they model self-discipline to their children. As children fast, they can gain the confidence that comes with knowing that they *can* say no.

Parents also help motivate children to exercise self-control as they verbalize their expectations for behavior. Despite the trappings of "coolness," deep down inside adolescents want to meet their parents' expectations. They may rebel. They may try to disown their parents. But if they know they are loved, your expectations of them often turn out to be self-fulfilling prophecies.

If Mom gives up hope of having a virtuous daughter and says, "Aw, nobody's a virgin these days anyway," her daughter is likely to allow herself to be used sexually. But if Mom and especially Dad make it clear that they expect virtuous behavior, teens are apt to try to meet those expectations.

Only parents can really teach self-control—though the church must reinforce the message and society should not undermine it. Only parents have the influence to motivate their kids to rise above the crowd—and just say no. ■

Can Parents Prevent Teen Drug Abuse?

Behind the teen drug problem is a "people problem" that parents can work to resolve in their own family.

Robert Bevans-Kerr

"If Dad doesn't do anything for me, then I won't do anything for him. I won't go to school." These are the words of Steve, a fifteen-year-old eighth grader, who attended school twenty days out of a possible ninety. Because of his truancy Steve was referred to me when I worked as a drug and alcohol prevention specialist.

Steve is growing up in a rural setting, living with his father, step-mother, brother (fourteen), and sister (eighteen). He first used marijuana at age ten, when his step-sister, age twenty-eight, shared a joint with him. He began using alcohol at age thirteen, and by the time he was fifteen, Steve had experimented with speed, acid, hashish, and cocaine. He says that 90 percent of his friends use drugs. Steve has also been arrested four times for crimes—including burglary, breaking and entering, and possession of marijuana. When he turns sixteen, he plans to drop out of school.

While Steve is not the norm, his is by no means an infrequent story. Although according to some recent studies, teen drug use has decreased statistically, the drug problem remains a serious threat. Parents should be concerned about their kids and watch out for any signs of drug use.

Studies indicate that in 1985, 61 percent of high school seniors had used drugs and that one out of every six thirteen-year-olds had used marijuana. The physical, social, and mental damage caused by such behavior cannot be ignored. When a child is found to be using drugs or alcohol,

continued on next page

Facing Teen Alcohol and Drug Abuse

No family is safe from the relentless danger of alcohol and drug abuse. Parents must take preventative steps and be prepared to act if necessary.

- Form your children in relying on God and his power—not just their own limited willpower. When they are faced with a difficult choice or a seemingly insurmountable problem, teach them to tap into the spiritual power available to them in Jesus Christ.
- Candidly admit to yourself that teen substance abuse *may* strike your family and is beyond your control. You, too, need to tap into the power that comes from Jesus Christ.
- Get educated about alcohol/drugs. Extensive information is available at your public library or local social service agencies.

continued on next page

parents should get professional help. Without it people cannot normally overcome any addiction. However, parents must do more than send teenagers who become substance abusers to counselors, expecting them to cure the problem.

Before there is a drug problem there is a people problem. Although there are a variety of motivations for teen drug usage, ranging from curiosity to self-destructive behavior, I think the real deep reasons kids turn to drugs are low self-esteem and lack of acceptance by others. My experience as an addictions counselor convinced me that a holistic approach—a family and community effort—is needed if we are going to effectively treat and prevent addiction among our youngsters. When communities, churches, and families promote healthy relationships, good communication, and positive self-esteem in our youth, then there is hope.

- Teach your family, including young children, about the dangers of substance abuse.
- Begin early to teach the family about the immorality of drunkenness and getting high. Train children in self-control.
- Have definite rules for any use of alcohol and pre-scription drugs in the family. Rules apply, of course, to parents as well as kids.
- If you or your spouse have a substance abuse problem, get help. For the alcoholic or addict, Alcoholics Anonymous is a good place to start. For the family of an afflicted person, Al-Anon offers help. Local chapters should be listed in your telephone directory.
- Watch for signs that a child might be using alcohol or other drugs. These include loss of interest in school or favorite pastimes, absence of motivation, sudden slippage in school grades, frequent inexplicable mood shifts and/or drowsiness, dramatic change in eating habits, leaving long-time friends for new ones, skipping classes or days from school, patterns of deceit

Parents, community and church leaders, and others who serve kids as role models can make a difference. Ask yourself the following questions:

- Do I recognize and acknowledge my own addictions, especially any unhealthy drug use?
- Am I willing to seek help and support from others?
- How do I foster good communication in my family and other social environments?
- Do I accept my child's strengths and weaknesses and allow him or her to express feelings in a healthy way?
- What do I do to build positive self-esteem for my family members?

Answering these questions and acting to change our behavior where necessary can help correct the people

continued on next page

and manipulative behavior, and possession of alcohol or drug-related paraphernalia.

- If you suspect a child is experimenting with or using alcohol and/or other drugs, do everything you can to keep communication open. Then get help.
- Excellent sources of help and information are parents who have had to deal with teen drug/alcohol problems. Talk to as many as you can to figure out your best course of action.
- Among many helpful books, an outstanding resource is Dick Schaefer, *Choices & Consequences: What to Do When a Teenager Uses Alcohol/Drugs* (Minneapolis: Johnson Institute Books, 1987).
- Nothing will drive you to your knees faster and harder than a teenager in trouble. That's a good posture for prevention, too. If you haven't begun to *pray daily* for each of your children, start now. God loves your kids more than you do and will answer your prayers for them.

Bert Ghezzi

problem which exists in our society.

Parents must acknowledge that drug addiction is not just a problem of youth. It is our problem. We are called first to heal the brokenness of our own lives and to support each other in this process. If parents are chemically addicted, they must get help and break out of the drug trap, in order to really help their kids get free and stay free.

Since communication is learned behavior, we can take steps to improve the way we express our ideas and feelings, as well as the way we listen to the ideas and feelings of others, especially our children. The key is to listen to our children so that they will talk to us and to speak to them in ways that get them to listen to us. Do a quick check of your communication with these questions:

- When I talk to my child do I resort to unhealthy modes of speech, like threats, nagging, or blaming?
- Do I ignore his or her concerns or refuse to deal with them?
- Am I sensitive to the tone of voice and expression when my child is trying to tell me something?
- Do I really take my child seriously when he or she opens up and wants to talk?

Good communication skills begin with attentiveness and respect for others. Children will learn to respect themselves when we respect them, so our good communication can help to build their positive self-esteem.

Given the condition of our society, no parent can guarantee that his child will avoid involvement with drugs. However, solving the people problem in our families can reduce the danger and provide a way of helping a child who has the misfortune of becoming a substance abuser. ■

Think, Pray, & Act

TEACHING KIDS CATHOLIC MORALITY

FOR REFLECTION AND DISCUSSION

1. How can guilt be a healthy experience for our children? (See articles by Blattner and Ranieri.)
2. Why can we expect kids to understand right and wrong? (See article by Blattner.)
3. What can a parent do to teach kids morality? (See article by Ranieri.)
4. How much sex education should parents give their kids, and when? (See article by Marshner.)
5. What can parents do to help prevent kids from using alcohol and other drugs? (See articles by Bevans-Kerr and Ghezzi.)

TAKING STOCK

Evaluate how well you are doing in teaching Catholic morality to your children. Review your own behavior and your approach to discipline. For help, refer to the articles by Ranieri and Blattner. Considering the following questions may help:

1. Your Behavior:

- Do my children witness me doing anything I have told them it was wrong to do? (For example, do I curse at other drivers? Do I get high on alcohol or drugs? Do I lie my way out of difficulties? And so on.)

- What good habits do I have that my children can imitate?
- Do I try to do the loving thing in every situation? (See article by Ranieri.)
- When I do something wrong, do I set a good example by dealing honestly with my sin and setting it right?
- Do I make use of the sacrament of reconciliation?

2. Your Discipline:

- Do I have a consistent way of correcting and punishing my child's wrongdoing?
- Is there a clear and short list of rules the children know they must not break? (For example, they must obey God's commandments, in particular, always obeying their parents, never lying, and never deliberately hurting anyone.)
- Do I use discipline as a way of teaching my children how to handle their sin? (Do I teach them about how sin offends God, about God's love and forgiveness, and about how to get reconciled with God and others?)

PLAN FOR ACTION

1. Your Behavior:

Review your answers to the questions in **Taking Stock.**

a. Is there some small decision you could make that would help you do a better job of teaching your kids morality? Try to do it. (For example, honestly admitting when you're wrong and saying you're sorry.)

b. Identify what change in your life would make the biggest improvement in training your children in morality. Consider what it would take to make the change. If you are willing to change in some major way, get the honest perspective and help of another person you trust. If you or your spouse have a serious personal problem, such as addiction or abuse, you need professional help. Your parish or Catholic Social Services can refer you.

2. Your Discipline:

a. Think through your expectations and your punishments for wrongdoing, being sure they suit the age of your kids.
b. Write a simple statement of your plan for family discipline. Of course, couples must agree on the policy in every detail.
c. Introduce or explain again to the family your approach to discipline. Use the discussion as a chance to teach the children about sin, offending God, God's love and forgiveness, and reconciliation. Refer to the articles by Blattner and Ranieri for help.
d. Apply the policy consistently and lovingly.

ACTIVITY

Have a Family Discussion or a one-on-one discussion with a child on an important moral issue or question. Select a topic the family or child will regard as important to them.

- For a family of children ages ten and under, consider pro-life issues. Use article by Schwartz in the next chapter as a resource.
- For older kids, discuss premarital sex. Refer to article by Marshner for ideas.

Remember to have a discussion, you must *listen* to the other parties and give reasons for what you say.

RESOURCES

- Jim Auer, *What's Right?: A Teenager's Guide to Christian Living* (Liguori).
- Julia Duin, *Purity Makes the Heart Grow Stronger* (Servant).
- Bert Ghezzi, *Transforming Problems* (Servant).
- Jeanine Timko Leichner, *Making Things Right: The Sacrament of Reconciliation* (Our Sunday Visitor).
- Carol Luebering, *The Forgiving Family: First Steps to Reconciliation* (Liguori).
- Connie Marshner, *Decent Exposure: How to Teach Your Children About Sex* (Wolgemuth & Hyatt).
- Ralph Martin, *Called to Holiness* (Servant).
- David Rosage, *What Scripture Says About God's Love* (Servant).
- Michael Scanlan, T.O.R., *Repentance: A Guide to Receiving God's Forgiveness* (Servant).
- Dick Schaefer, *Choices & Consequences; What to Do When a Teenager Uses Alcohol/Drugs* (Johnson Institute Books).
- *The Ten Commandments for Children* (Regina Press).
- Ken Wilson, *The Obedient Child: A Practical Guide for Training Young Children in Confidence, Character, and Love of God* (Servant).

NINE

Communicating a Catholic Approach to the World

We and our children are called to bring a Catholic Christian influence to bear on our society. Let's show them how while they're young.

Raising Kids with Concern for Social Justice

Why we must teach our kids social justice and how to get started.

James D. Manney

My wife, Sue, and I don't *talk* to our children very much about social justice, the needs of the poor, and the principles of service to others. These ideas are too abstract for small children, "boring" and "preachy" to older ones. However, we think about them a lot and try to build them into our family life. Our concern has directed major choices that have shaped our family—like our decision in 1972 to move into a predominantly black neighborhood. Yes, it was easier to afford a house in this "less-desirable" neighborhood, but we had also made a decision to raise our children among people of different races and to give them a concern for the needy.

"Social justice" can be a troublesome term. That's okay. The existence of poor, needy, confused, oppressed, troubled, and exploited people *should* trouble us. And any serious effort to raise Catholic children must include training in the necessity of reaching out to them with Christ's love and Christ's mercy.

Yet, in doing this, we are bound to get involved in a number of tricky questions and unclear choices.

These are some of them.

"What Are We Talking about, Anyway?" Good question. Just what *are* we talking about when we talk about raising children to have a concern for social justice? Do we mean educating our kids about the nuances of weapons systems, great power conflict, welfare policy, civil rights, and housing problems? And what does "concern" mean? Having the right ideas? Voting for the right political candidates? Writing checks to charitable organizations? Selling all you have and giving to the poor?

Concern for social justice can and does mean all these things. But the most helpful answer for most parents is to change one word in the question. The question isn't *what* are we talking about? but *who* are we talking about? In our town, *who* is in so much trouble that they need some kind of help?

No one will have trouble coming up with a distressingly long list. Here's a partial one:

- single parents with small children;
- prisoners;
- recovering and practicing addicts and alcoholics;
- homeless people;
- former patients with mental illness who have been released;

- teenagers on the run from abusive parents and step-parents;
- immigrants;
- residents of nursing homes;
- women with crisis pregnancies;
- AIDS patients;
- other hospitalized patients and their families.

Jesus said, "the poor you will always have with you." These are the people whom we must teach our children to love and to learn from. As they grow up, our children will learn about the social systems, cultural norms, and public policies that are implicated in the suffering we see around us. But it's important to begin with the simple need.

One cynical machine boss said, "All politics is local." For kids and families, "All charity is local, too."

Let's Not Reduce the Problem to Politics. Yes, let's not. I think it's a problem that the term "social justice" has acquired a strong political connotation with both a leftist and a rightist twist.

Somehow we've got the idea that people who work for social justice are typically leftists concerned primarily with the federal government's foreign and domestic policies, with the emphasis on government's failures and the prospect that a new government would do better. Or we think they're right-wing activists, concerned for abortion, official secularism in the public schools, pornography, and other "family" issues commonly identified with the label "Christian New Right."

Let's drop as many of these political associations as we can. Social justice does not mean bashing the man in the White House. Pro-life and pro-family activism does not mean lining up conservative Christians for some candidate's next campaign. The vast majority of outreach to those in need can be conducted without serious involvement in partisan politics or serious political disagreement.

Republicans and Democrats can work together emptying the bed pans of AIDS patients without battling over political issues.

Of course we can't stay out of politics completely. Nor should we. Persistent, troubling conditions that affect many people—homelessness, abortion, drugs, and the like—have a way of working their way onto the public political agenda. They should. Some elements of these problems can only be properly addressed through politics.

But many dimensions of these problems are best served by individual Christians reaching out with Christ's love to other individuals. These are the dimensions we should show our children.

The Problems Are Too Big. If you seriously get involved in the needs of other people, weariness and depression are likely to set in eventually. Consider the following:

- "We can't do anything about homelessness. The forces that tear families apart and throw people out of work are bigger than we are."
- "I don't know whether I'm up for twenty more years of pro-life work. The battles over legal abortion will be going on long after I'm dead."
- "When I started working in a soup kitchen, the big drug was alcohol. Then it was heroin. Now it is crack. Where will it end?"

It won't. Remember, the poor we will always have with us. This is a miserable, unwelcome fact. Even the most stalwart ministers to the poor are frequently tempted to give up. The temptation is even stronger for parents who are trying to raise their children with a godly commitment to social justice. We are bred to strive for success. But this work presents one failure after another. We like to solve problems; the poor and the needy present a never-ending succession of problems that never end and are never quite solved.

We need to put aside the grand problem-solving mentality to get involved with those in need. We are dealing with *people*, not problems. If our goals are properly modest—getting an old man to the doctor, helping an illiterate child learn to read, collecting nursery furniture for a pregnant woman who has decided to give birth to her child rather than getting an abortion—we can make a difference.

Some Practical Pointers

Here are a few key principles for introducing kids to social concern. They are based on my own experience and that of some friends.

1. Make It as Personal as Possible. A key to teaching your children about the importance of a huge abstraction such as "social justice" is to get them involved with specific *people* who have needs. The old lady who needs someone to take her to the doctor. The kid who needs some tutoring to keep up with his reading group. The man with multiple sclerosis who needs someone to help him live in his apartment and stay out of an institution.

2. Make Sure Your Work Serves the Needs of the Receiver, not the Giver. The classic example of the self-serving gesture is donating Thanksgiving turkeys to local poor people. Another is the youth group's pre-Christmas concert at the local nursing home.

These are harmless gestures, but it's hard to see how much good they do for the people they are intended for. The needy family has to worry about food for the 364 days between Thanksgivings and the good feelings generated by Christmas carols on December 21 won't carry lonely old folks very far into the new year.

Our service has to be based on a realistic judgment about the real needs of the people being served.

Service must also be based on motives other than guilt. We must serve other people because God loves them and because he has given us something to share.

3. Learn Something from the Poor and Needy. Close and repeated contact with people in some kind of distress can bring great insight and wisdom to the giver—to you and your family.

Many of them are spiritual lessons. We may labor under the illusion that we are in charge, that life is what we make it, and that we can control what happens. The poor and sick and needy know better than most how false this really is. God is in charge and life is what **he** makes of it.

Have difficulty living in faith? Get to know some people for whom every day is a gift from God.

This is not to romanticize the poor. They are afflicted by sin just as everyone is. But it is a common experience of those who minister to those in serious need—from Mother Teresa and her Missionaries of Charity to the people in your parish who volunteer their time—that they seem to benefit from the experience more than those they serve.

I know a young couple in New Jersey who go to Manhattan every Monday to work with young people at Covenant House, the shelter for homeless young people. Every week they talk to and pray with kids whose lives are terribly afflicted. More than half have been exposed to the AIDS virus. Many have been on drugs. Many have been involved in prostitution. My friends share hope with them. They try to give them faith, to point the way to a better, more righteous way of life.

The result.

"I honestly believe we get more out of it than they do," says John.

"It builds *our* faith," says Debbie, his wife. "I can't wait to get there every week."

One other lesson: if you have any idea that the poor and

needy are somehow responsible for their own condition, an outreach to these people will convince you otherwise. One of the most destructive illusions of modern middle-class life is the notion that we acquire what we have by our own pluck, intelligence, and hard work.

Many plucky, intelligent, and hard working people live on the edge of starvation. Many ignorant and lazy people have great wealth. Those who live in advanced industrial civilizations are going to reap greater rewards for their efforts than those who don't.

God gave us what we have. We are blessed. That's *why* we need to take care of others.

4. *Pray for a Total Solution. Work for a Partial One.* We hunger for total solutions. Something in our minds craves them. Poverty in Africa. The arms race. Drugs. Hunger in the Caribbean. The solutions to these problems involve more time than we have, more people than we know, more resources than we can imagine. Let's pray for them. And let's concern ourselves about the policy issues to the extent that we can.

Meanwhile, let's serve the needy and hungry and suffering people that the Lord sends our way without asking too many questions. The alcoholic we feed will drink again. The hungry person will get hungry again. The drug addict may never stop using. The AIDS patient is going to die. The people in Haiti and Honduras and Ethiopia and Bangladesh have many needs—complicated, intertwined, maddening needs. We can only meet some of them.

This seemed to be Jesus' way in the New Testament. He did not solve the hunger problem in Judea; he didn't stamp out leprosy; he didn't overthrow a brutal and corrupt government. Instead, he fed the hungry people and healed the sick—when they came to him.

And he founded a kingdom, in which his followers did the same. ■

Six Suggestions for Raising Pro-Life Children

We cannot force our kids to hold pro-life convictions, but we can instill in them a deep respect for life.

Michael Schwartz

According to a half-serious joke, the pro-life cause is bound to be successful in the long run because pro-life people are the only ones having children.

Leaving aside the mathematics of this proposition, one reason why it is a joke instead of a prediction is that there is no way we can be sure our children will agree with us. All the pro-abortionists, after all, are children or grandchildren of people who took it for granted that abortion was a barbarous crime. A pro-life attitude is obviously not hereditary.

Our children, because they are made in the image and likeness of God, are endowed with free will. As they grow older, they will make their own decisions about what they believe and how they will live.

We cannot force them to share our pro-life convictions any more than we can force them to be good Catholics. What we can do, and what we must do if we take our parental responsibilities seriously, is to foster in them a spirit of respect for life.

To a large extent, this is simply identical with imparting a genuine Christian faith to our children, since the Christian spirit is pro-life. But there are a few specific points we might bear in mind as we raise our children in this materialistic, death-worshiping culture of ours.

1. Be a Pro-Life Person Yourself in a Way Your Children Can See. Nothing impresses a child, or anyone else for that matter, better than good example.

This does not mean we are all obliged to do sidewalk counseling or open our homes to an unwed mother or campaign for pro-life candidates. Those are all excellent things to do, but not everyone is called to active forms of pro-life witness. We should, however, do whatever we can to aid the right-to-life movement with our financial contributions, our time, our prayers and our personal interest and commitment. And, on reflection, most of us would have to admit we could be doing more.

In day-to-day life, too, we need to keep our pro-life values visible. How often, for instance, when we hear that someone is pregnant, do we respond with sympathy instead of congratulations? Even as a joke, that sends a bad message. If the pregnancy involves a problem (husband out of work, no husband, illness, and so on), then the problem deserves our sympathy and, if possible, our help. But the baby is *not* the problem. The baby *is* a gift from God.

2. Teach Your Children Why Life Is Sacred. I can remember my mother telling me that I was God's child lent to her for a time and that it was her responsibility to give me back to God ready to serve him. This was a powerful truth. It made me aware of my own value as the object of God's immediate and personal concern, and it helped me to see that everyone else was loved by God just as much. It also impressed me with what a holy vocation parenthood is. This is a truth we can all share in some way with our children.

3. Foster in Your Children a Sense of Courage in the Truth. Teach them to form convictions and to live by them. Everyone encounters peer pressure, not just teenagers. We all conform, to a certain extent, with what is fashionable. But we have to be clear, and we have to make sure our children are clear about the difference between fashion and principle. It is always very hard to stand against the tide, but a person who compromises on matters of principle is lacking in honor and self-respect. Firmness in adhering to that truth gives a person dignity.

4. *Inspire in Your Children Fidelity to the Church as the Infallible Source of Guidance.* The gift of faith is our greatest treasure, in part because, as Chesterton noted, it saves us from "the awful disgrace of being a child of our times." The teachings of the church are an absolutely reliable guide to what we should believe and how we should live, and as long as we receive that guidance humbly and follow it honestly, we can be certain that we are not falling into error.

When the disciples left Jesus because they thought his teaching was too hard, he turned to Peter and asked, "What about you? Do you want to go away too?" And Peter answered, "Lord, to whom shall we go? You have the words of eternal life." Jesus continues to give us those "words of eternal life" through his church, which is his extension in time and space.

5. *Let Your Children Know that Success in Life Does not Consist in Making a Lot of Money or Getting Good Grades or Having Many Friends.* All these things are good, but they are not the reason why we are here. The real goal we have to instill in our children is to grow in virtue and in love for God and our neighbor. We live in a tremendously materialistic culture, and naturally, we want our children to be as successful as possible in this life. But we must never lose sight of priorities. We have to teach our children, especially by our own example, to be ready to make sacrifices for the sake of justice and charity.

6. *Let Your Children Know that Life Itself Is Under Attack.* Those of us who are Christians in this society have a special mission to stand up for the sacredness of life. The world in which our children are growing up is one which shows a contempt for life in many ways. The gross evils of abortion and euthanasia involve the actual killing of those who are deemed inconvenient.

But other social evils such as racism or contempt for the handicapped or the elderly or the foreigner also imply a depersonalization that violates human dignity. We need to discuss these issues with our children and steer them away from anti-life attitudes they may pick up. Above all, let's keep these concerns present in our family prayer. Children who learn to pray for others, even those who might be thought of as enemies, are not likely to learn to hate. And children who learn love instead of hate will grow up with a strong sense of respect for life. ■

What Parents Can Do about Teen Music

We can affirm what is good in our teens' culture, teach them how to discern the evil there, and help them to avoid it.

Bert Ghezzi

I was fifteen, and my cousin Frank was fourteen. We had spent the better part of two rainy days cooped up in a vacation cottage listening to our collection of 45s. Repeatedly, we played the songs of Bill Haley, Fats Domino, and Elvis Presley. My uncle, who was trapped indoors with us, finally had enough.

"How can you guys stand that noise?" he asked. He was determined that we hear some "good music" sung by his favorite, Frank Sinatra. We were not impressed.

It is a rule of modern culture that teens are not supposed to like their parents' music and vice versa. If our parents had liked the new rock sound of the mid-1950s, we would probably have found something they couldn't stand.

Teen music celebrates our passage from childhood into adolescence, our entry into the youth culture. Adolescents are trying their best to assume a new identity, one that is distinct from their parents. They choose hairstyles, clothes, speech, music, and other externals that defy their parents' sense of good taste.

Teens adopt the trappings of the youth culture as an expression of independence, testing how far parents will let them go. Most just want to be different, not rebellious. While my cousin and I liked Bill Haley and the Comets' revolutionary song "Rock Around the Clock," which has been called the Marseillaise of rock 'n' roll, we did not regard it as an act of defiance. We just enjoyed the music.

Frank Sinatra was also something of an upstart in his day. My uncle thought he was tops, but I wonder what my grandma thought of him? I bet she wished she could get recordings from Italy so she could let her son hear what really "good music" was like.

A Rite of Passage with Significant Differences. While I see the similarities between my youth culture of the 1950s and that of the 1980s, I also recognize significant differences. Accelerating social changes subject today's young people to more pressures than most of us knew. Divorce, for example, has shattered countless families, introducing many children to the pain of rejection, loneliness, and instability.

Technological advances and affluence have also greatly complicated matters. I spoke a short time ago to a former high-school principal who had retired in the mid '60s. He said he got out just as the pill and drugs were coming in. "Kids before got a little frisky and caused some trouble, but they were just having fun. The pill and drugs made it different; they made it hard."

Contemporary teen music for the most part proclaims the ideals of a youth culture that conflicts with Christianity. The next time you have a chance, listen to the words of the Top-40 songs. With the exception of a few nonsense novelty songs, most lyrics are about boy-girl relationships. They presume full sexual expression, speak about sleeping together, and spending the night together or "doing *it.*"

Here is a list of sexual acts specified in Top-40's songs:

- The group Ready for the World sings about fornication in "Oh, Sheila"; in "Digital Display" a boy fondles a girl's breasts until his "digit displays"; in "Girl Tonight" the boy patiently coaxes the girl to have intercourse, touching her genitally to assure her that she's ready.
- Prince in "Darling Niki" and Cyndi Lauper in "She Bop" sing about masturbation.
- And Prince in "Sister" sings about incest, saying that it is "everything it's said to be."

Hard rock and heavy metal groups such as Motley Crue, Led Zeppelin, Metallica, Metal Church, and others add violence to this mix. They sing about rebellion against parents and all authority, drug abuse, inflicting pain, murder, and committing suicide. Some groups such as Black Sabbath have plunged into the occult with songs that are blasphemous and that exalt Satan.

True, many kids listen to rock songs because the sound makes them feel good, and they pay little attention to the words. For example, some young people who have listened to the songs many times will be as shocked as you are when they read the sexually explicit lyrics. But this is the context they live in, and words like these beat in their brains up to four to six hours every day.

A New Twist: The Rock Video. Cable television and some networks bring video versions of teen songs into your living room. For the most part, these are videos of groups in concert, interspersed frenetically with weird or nonsensical cinematography. Some of it is innocuous and some is wholesome, but most is not. Have you seen Van Halen's video "Hot For Teacher"? The group leads what appear to be thirteen-year-olds in watching a teacher strip to a bikini and dance suggestively. Twisted Sister has made videos featuring violence, including a scene where a son throws his father against doors, down a flight of stairs, and through a window. Some videos highlight sexual violence, including whipping and bondage. The Meese Commission on Pornography was alarmed enough by some teen music to include in its recommendations that parents monitor their children's listening and viewing.

Music is not something our teens take casually. It is a celebration of the youth culture, a way of life they find irresistibly attractive. That means parents cannot take it casually either. Our desire to do something about teen music is right, but what to do is the question.

What You Can Do

When we decide to tackle teen music, we need perspective before we act. Our real frustration may be with our own inability to deal with what our teens are going through. They are confused by physical and emotional changes that both excite and frighten them. They become like strangers to us, and often we find ourselves unable to understand or to help them.

Lashing out against rock music may bring us relief by venting our frustration, but it may also camouflage our failure to face the deeper problems involved in helping our kids through these difficult years. We should deal with teen music, but we should not make it a scapegoat for our own weaknesses. Sometimes we should grapple first with other, bigger problems, temporarily setting aside the matter of music.

Some parents make a frontal assault against rock music, banning it completely. This approach works best when the teens identify strongly with their parents' values or when they have the support of peers in like-minded families.

However, banning teen music does not mean parents can safely ignore it. We can keep teen music out of our homes, but we cannot completely control it. Unless we take Mark Twain's advice and confine our adolescents in sealed boxes, they will be immersed in teen music on the street, on the bus, in school, in shops, in friend's homes—everywhere. So parents who choose to forbid rock music need to be vigilant and constantly refresh their kids' commitment to the approach.

All parents should view teen music as an opportunity to teach their kids how to sort out the good from the evil in their culture. I suggest that we help our kids evaluate their music by communicating with them about it and that we control it by setting reasonable limits. We should consider building the following elements into our approach:

1. Parents Should Learn to Appreciate What's Good in the Youth Culture. This means expressing their approval for it to their teens. Some songs are wholesome. Once I told my kids that I thought the songs "Caravan of Love," which advocates brotherhood, and "Stand by Me," which promotes loyalty, were good songs. Whenever tunes such as these air, someone always says, "There's Dad's favorite song." Showing appreciation for something that our teenagers value *strengthens* our relationship with them. It says we *respect* them and that means a great deal to them.

2. Parents Should Listen to Music with Their Teens and Discuss It with Them. We should ask them why they like a song, or if they understand or agree with the lyrics. We should listen to them, so that we really are having a discussion and not giving a lecture.

Discussing a song with objectionable content is a chance to explain our concern about the lifestyle celebrated in teen music. Once, for example, a fifteen-year-old was listening to a song about a boy seducing a girl. I asked him if he knew what the song was about, and I quoted the offensive part of the lyrics to him. "Well, it's good soul music," he said, "but you're right, the words aren't good."

3. Parents Should Set Reasonable Guidelines to Regulate Teen's Music Consumption. I recommend some version of the following list:

- Listening to teen music can be permitted, but music with sexually explicit or violent lyrics ought not to be allowed in the house. We should establish the policy that any offensive material that slips in inadvertently will be returned to its source.

In November 1985, the Parents Music Resource Center (PMRC) and the National Parents and Teachers Association got twenty major recording companies to agree to place warning labels or copies of lyrics on recordings with explicit sex, violence, or drug use. Parents should watch for such warning labels, but since many companies do not provide them, reading lyrics is the only sure test. (For assistance or information, write to PMRC, 1500 Arlington Blvd., Arlington, VA 22209.)

- We should specify when and where teen music may be played. For example, no radio until homework is completed. Respect for others may dictate limiting teen music to certain rooms and certain times of day.

- The best way to regulate viewing music videos is not to subscribe to cable networks that carry them. So many music videos are offensive or weird that the damage they do to the spirit, the mind, and good taste is incalculable.

What about parties, dances, and rock concerts? Parents should understand that in these contexts teen music performs a kind of "evangelistic" function, enticing kids to sample other questionable elements of the youth culture.

Parents who don't want their thirteen-year-olds learning to dance to songs about sexual intercourse should investigate events before allowing them to attend. We should feel free to discuss with other parents their plans for parties which their kids invite ours to attend. Before letting teenagers go to dances, we should go to one ourselves or even volunteer to be chaperones. If your teenager wants to go to a rock concert, offer to take him or her once so you can see for yourself what goes on and evaluate it together.

You will not very easily apply the limits discussed here to older teenagers whose musical tastes have never been supervised before. You can, however, discuss their music with them, acknowledging what is good and explaining your objections to what is bad. We should keep lines of communication open with older teens so we can patiently and lovingly draw them to Christ.

Entrusting all of our teenagers to the Lord is the most effective way of protecting them from evil influences. But remember, even prayer does not excuse us from our responsibility of helping them learn to fight the temptations of their world. ∎

Family Ties with Limits on TV Viewing

*Setting limits on television time is a difficult
yet necessary task for today's Christian parents.*

Mary Ann Kuharski

Most parents grew up with television, a factor which can make it more difficult for them to monitor their own children's TV viewing. Also television in the late forties and fifties was limited largely to wholesome family entertainment. Not anymore. TV of the eighties assures viewers of around-the-clock viewing. The definition of family has broadened to include the divorced, the blended family, the unmarried, and active homosexual partners.

The viewer of today receives an endless display of promiscuity, eccentricity, and mediocrity (not to mention the double message of the contraceptive and AIDS prevention ads). We've come a long way from yesteryear. Today the average viewer watches six hours of television per day. TV-watching children today will witness more than fifteen thousand killings before they reach the age of sixteen. Is it any wonder they are complacent about abortion, mercy killing, and infanticide?

Moral Influences. Although we limit TV in our home, I recently walked in on my children (ages two to eighteen) engrossed in a Sunday evening thirty-minute sitcom. I was just in time to see a pretty young girl snuggle up to her bashful pursuer and ask, "Would you like to kiss me? Would you like to rip off all my clothes and have sex with me?" The TV response was five seconds of canned laughter at which my younger children looked on in confusion.

Normally we would think of such a description as forced rape. Hardly a laughing matter. And hardly a notion parents would want embedded in their children's minds. How far we've gone from the wholesome family entertainment once offered during prime time.

TV-watching children today will witness more than fifteen thousand killings before they reach the age of sixteen.

Unlimited TV watching is an irresistible lure and can stifle young and curious minds. Concerned Christian parents have a moral obligation to love their children enough to limit their viewing habits.

Setting Limits

Through trial and error our family has used the following rules as our guides. Perhaps they will be helpful to other parents in their attempts to curtail and control that addictive instrument fondly called television.

1. Establish Your Authority Now. Children must realize that the television belongs to the parents. Shows chosen and the number of viewing hours are determined by Mom and Dad.

2. Children Should Ask Before Watching. Do not allow them to turn on the TV automatically. The practice of asking reminds youngsters that the tube is not at their discretion.

This rule prevents them from watching out of boredom, with no thought as to what is being aired.

3. *Set Your Standards and Keep Them.* At our house no daytime television is allowed except Mister Rogers' Neighborhood or Sesame Street in the winter months.

We limit TV viewing to two hours after dinner time, with news shows or specials approved by us as the exceptions.

4. *Your Home Is Your Castle.* Your home and what happens in it depends upon you. If you find a movie or show distasteful, vulgar, or offensive, you have automatic veto power. Don't let teens or young adults who argue about their rights bully you. Gently but firmly remind them that until they are in their own home, they have no right to air a program you consider objectionable.

5. *Outlaw Personal TVs.* Today's American family is vulnerable to outside influences. The more isolated members become, the easier it is to build walls. One young couple thought they did their preteen boys a favor by giving them a TV set for their room. Such decisions isolate children and create unlimited and unhealthy viewing habits. The more a youngster learns to consider, compromise, and bend to the wishes of others, the less self-centered he or she will be.

6. *Television—a Privilege, not a Pacifier.* TV is a sophisticated instrument made for entertainment and educational use. Never use it as a baby-sitter or pacifier to keep rowdy or rambunctious kids in control. Even the most boisterous youngster will respond if encouraged to play constructively. Patience, praise, and early training are the key in helping a child feel appreciated, instead of pacified.

7. *Set the Example.* If you are in the habit of plopping your tired body and mind in front of the tube each evening, remember that your actions speak louder than your words. You cannot ask something difficult of your children unless you are willing to break the pattern in your own life. Limit your own viewing to informative, educational, and truly entertaining programs.

8. Sunshine and Fresh Air Take Precedence. We live in Minnesota where the winter months bring early darkness and weather too cold for playing outside. During this season, our TV gets the most use. When spring appears, we reject even the most popular programming for the backyard swing set, a walk around the block, bike riding, reading, or outdoor activity.

9. Substitute Adventure for Boredom. To help make the transition easier, read a book, play a board or card game, or go for a walk with your children. Don't worry about be-

continued on next page

Using Television to Teach Christian Values

Have you ever watched a child deeply involved in an adventure-packed television story? Many actually warn a character of danger or clench their fists to help in a fight. Comments and involvement are natural additions to what we experience on television. Parents who are aware of this can act as a catalyst in talking about the values presented through the character's actions.

The parent can ask clarifying questions during commercials. How would you feel if you were that boy? What would you do next in his place? Did anything like that

continued on next page

coming television's permanent replacement or having to create daily activities for them. Their need of you will diminish as they begin to create their own entertainment. Meanwhile, it's a chance to capture some tender and fun moments together.

10. Make Sunday Night Family Night. Limiting your television viewing leaves free time for leisure. Sunday is a good time for Christian families to restore the concept of a family day. Having guests for dinner, going on picnics, or bringing out the family snapshot albums are activities that bring you and your children together. These memories will stay in your children's minds far longer than the most popular or longest running show. ■

ever happen to you? Another kind of question is appropriate at the end of the story. What part of the show did you like best? least? and why?

When using any of these questions, it is important to share your answers too, without insisting on being right. This gives children room to grapple with their own values and examine yours at the same time. Your values will affect your child, especially if they are reflected in daily life. But don't be surprised if an older child points out a discrepancy between your spoken and lived values. Family discussions are a good place to admit that we are not perfect. So why should we expect our children to be? All of us are struggling towards goodness together.

John and Therese Boucher

Think, Pray, & Act

CATHOLICS AND THE WORLD

FOR REFLECTION AND DISCUSSION

1. Why must we instill in our children a concern for social justice? (See articles by Manney and Schwartz.)
2. How can we give our children a Catholic concern for social justice? (See articles by Manney and Schwartz.)
3. How can parents teach teens to distinguish good from bad in the youth culture? (See article by Ghezzi.)
4. What attitudes and controls should parents have regarding teen music? (See article by Ghezzi.)
5. Why should parents control family TV viewing? How can parents use television to teach Christian values? (See articles by Kuharski and the Bouchers.)

TAKING STOCK

Assess the way you and your family relate to the world around you. You may want to consider the following questions:

1. Your Attitudes and Actions:

- How familiar am I with Catholic teaching on social justice?
- Have I compared my attitudes on such questions as civil rights, care for the needy, economic justice, and so on with Catholic teaching?
- When was the last time I helped someone in need?

- Do I make any unwise or wrongful use of worldly things? (For example, am I irresponsible with money? Am I addicted to TV viewing? Do I make use of immoral entertainments?)

2. Your Family:

- What have you done to teach your children Catholic approaches to the world?
- What control do you have over your child's relationship to the youth culture?
- Have you ever discussed social issues with your child?
- Has your family ever helped another family in need? How?
- Have you placed any limits on TV viewing in your home? Have you made any positive use of TV in your family?

PLAN FOR ACTION

Using the articles by Kuharski and the Bouchers, develop a plan both to limit TV use in your home and to use it constructively. Be sure to take the following into account:

1. Keep your plan simple.
2. Make the limits reasonable (for example, no more than two hours total video—TV and games—per day).
3. Provide alternatives to help fill empty time. Have good books and games available.
4. Be sure you are not exempting yourself from the rules.
5. Select one wholesome and educational program each week. Watch the program with your kids and discuss it together.

ACTIVITY

1. As a family, survey the major social needs in your city. For example, hunger, homelessness, abortion, child abuse, prisoners, AIDS patients.
2. Select one area and study the need together. Use your local library and contact state and other social agencies for information.
3. Study the Catholic teaching on the area. For help, contact your parish, diocese, or Catholic Social Services.
4. Make each family member responsible for studying about a part of the topic and report back. Involve the children within the limits of their age and ability.
5. Find a need close to your neighborhood that your family could meet. These criteria will help you be successful:

    - You should look for *someone* to help, rather than an organization to give to or a place to staff. Meeting a person in need and helping them will have a deep effect on the whole family.
    - You should choose to do something you have the human resources to accomplish.
    - You should select a limited activity which the family can manage and one which does not have to continue for a long period.

RESOURCES

- Pope Paul VI, *Evangelization in the Modern World (Evangelii Nuntiandi)* (United States Catholic Conference).
- *The Beatitudes for Children* (Regina Press).
- Jim Auer, *10 Tough Issues for Teenagers* (Liguori).
- Virgil Gulker, *Help Is Just Around the Corner: How Love Inc. Mobilizes Care for the Needy* (Creation House).

TEN

Looking Back, Looking Ahead

Catholic parents can have hope for their children, as they see the faith and experience of others who have kept their kids close to God.

Returning to My Catholic Roots

A young Catholic who came back to the church describes four important ways to root kids in the faith.

Paul Lauer

I *could* tell you about being arrested at age thirteen for robbing houses—I wore handcuffs long before I wore aftershave. Or I could describe what it's like to spend ten years outside the church, dabbling in everything from drugs to women to Buddhism to "me-ism." Or maybe you'd prefer a short synopsis of those years I spent playing in a rock band? Well, I figure you've seen enough of that on TV already, right? Music, parties, breaking the law, leaving the church—so what else is new?

Well, quite a bit, really. So I'm glad you asked. You see, I'm now a twenty-seven-year-old practicing Catholic who four and a half years ago returned to the church; three and a half years ago quit his rock band and moved into the desert to become a saint; and one and a half years ago came down to earth and turned his parents' garage into the publishing "empire" of *Veritas* Catholic youth magazine.

An unheard of, miraculous conversion story? You bet. Just the way God always writes them. But was I really "knocked off my horse"? No. Was I visited by the angel Gabriel? Not that I recall. Was it a dream I had? No. I usually only dream about riding perfect waves on my surfboard.

My conversion story is really no more miraculous than the story God has already written for you or for the loved one you are trying to keep in—or bring back to—the church. And though I may not be one of God's *official* staff writers, I think I can show you everything you can possibly do to help make one of his "miraculous conversion" stories come about. . . .

1. The Challenge. I and others who have had a "miraculous conversion" were not converted because we were shown that what we were doing was wrong (nobody ever wants to hear that, eh?), but rather because we were shown that something else was *more right*. Instead of being forced to turn off to evil, we were invited to turn on to good.

Imagine that Hollywood with all its attractions represented life with all its sin and temptations. If I want to close Hollywood down, one method would be to get court injunctions and then bulldoze the seedy place to pieces. Sure, I would be done with all the attractions, but what would I be left with? A pile of rubble and neon lights—nothing to offer the hordes who come to Hollywood looking for action.

What if, instead, I build the most attractive and boldest club on Hollywood's strip? Without compromising my tastes, I create a club so unique, bold, and challenging that it outshines the rest. People are attracted to my club and begin to frequent it, until finally it becomes the place to be. Other clubs go out of business because their customers are coming to me and eventually I will be able to make all the other clubs annexes for mine.

Are you catching my drift? Though we must fight to tear down evil, we must work even harder building up good. Have you noticed how people like Mother Teresa take a constructive, instead of a destructive approach—addition instead of subtraction. That's important because God is addition, not subtraction. He died on the cross not to subtract life, but rather to add life to our hearts. Ever notice how the cross is a plus sign?

The bottom line is: energy and expansion come with youth and they will be used for good or for bad. We must challenge young people to channel their abundant energy for good, for God, for the church, and the world. And, believe me, we will never convince them to do so if what we have to offer them is not a challenge. Young people have enough energy to climb tall mountains of faith, hope, and love. If all we offer them are little mole hills, they'll simply go elsewhere for their challenges—to punk rock, drugs, or satanism.

2. *Common Ground.* How do we even begin to challenge our young people? We need some common ground—some level of communication. And this is the very thing we are missing today. We're a disconnected society. And it all started with the breakdown of the family unit. Never before have five people in the same family been able to sit in a room together for two hours and not say a word to each other. Now it's easy. Just put a TV in front of them. And the dinner table? Not necessary. Just nuke your frozen dinner when you get hungry and eat it solo. Then you can pop on your Walkman headphones and head for the solitude of your room. Mom and Dad won't be around tonight, anyway. They're both working late. . . .

Disconnected. Bad news. Parents and kids must start to have rapport. Do you understand your kids? When they do some crazy thing, do you patiently try to understand why? When Jesus at age twelve stayed behind at the temple, Mary did not scold, but simply asked why. Asking why gets at the cause of the problem instead of trying to doctor its effects.

We must give our lives as sure, solid ground for young people. A young person may go through dozens of stages, changes, beliefs, philosophies, experiments, and so on. At the end of it all he or she will remember what was constant in their lives—the love, the faith, the support we have shown them through the years. There would never have been a repentant prodigal son had he not had the hope of finding a forgiving father waiting back home.

3. Formation and the Sacraments. Next to love, our faith is the most important aspect of the solid ground we offer our youth. The richness of our faith enables us to to stretch our roots deep into the ground—into two thousand years of history and culture and tradition. How powerful this is!

Here's the key question: Are we rooting our kids in the faith? Do we teach them the history of the church? Do they know what it means to be Catholic, not just a generic-brand Christian? Have they ever heard the lives of the saints? Have they ever prayed the rosary? Do they understand the Eucharist? Do they know what the church teaches and why? We are cheating them if we have not rooted them in these things, since Catholic formation and the sacraments are sources of God's grace for us.

4. Prayer. God relies on us to assist him in his work of redemption. He has entrusted the salvation of youth to us. If we don't lead them to God, who in Aunt Jemima's kitchen will? When Jesus met the women on the way of the cross, he told them, "Don't weep for me. Weep for yourselves and your children." Well, are we weeping for them? Are we praying for them? Are we begging God for the grace of conversion for them?

And are we teaching our children to pray? Have we convinced them that prayer works? Do they see us praying? Sure, it's never easy—kids get fidgety, little fights break out, the phone rings. But Father Peyton was right, I think: "The family that prays together, stays together."

It was the prayers of my mother and grandmother that helped bring me back to the church. After my Irish grandmother died, I began to wear a Miraculous Medal in her memory. Well, folks, never doubt the power of the Virgin Mary. She's an expert at finding and bringing children back to the church. Within a month I received a call from an old friend—an accomplice in many crimes—who started telling me about the Catholic faith. Through conversations with him and others, it all came alive for me and soon I was back in the church. Just another *miraculous* conversion story!

What if you cover these four important areas and your young person does not seem to experience a conversion? You've tried to challenge them. You worked at having a common, solid ground. You've done your best to form them in the faith, the sacraments, and prayer. Still they look comatose when they sit through Sunday Mass.

Then what? Give up. That's right, give up. And I mean *really give* up—all the way up to heaven. Take your children's hearts and do what Mary and so many others have done: give them up to God. Put them in his hands.

Someone once asked Mother Teresa how she ever thought she could be successful when millions are starving and she is feeding only a few thousand. She said, "God did not call me to be successful, but to be faithful." So, never lose hope. Be positive. Stay faithful. Believe. Leave the rest to God, our Father, who never gives us less than the best. ■

Is It Your Fault If Your Kids Leave the Church?

After all is said and done,
keeping kids Catholic is God's work.

Dolores Curran

If there's one question I can count on hearing whenever I address a group of Catholic parents it's: "What do you do when your grown children leave the church?" While it's no longer asked with the furtiveness and shame it once was, it grabs the group's attention.

The answer is easy, "You pray and continue in your faith as usual. That's all you can do."

Letting Go. I firmly believe that there comes a time in all parents' lives when they have to hand their young adults over to God with: "We did the best with what you sent us, Lord. They're in your hands now. Lead them to you in whatever way you see fit."

And we parents have to accept that God's way may not be our way. It may mean a temporary or permanent lapse from Catholicism. It may mean that grown children will adopt a different denomination or none at all.

I've seen parents' own faith shaken when their young adults abandon active practice of the faith. I've seen others scourge themselves for years because they failed to produce "Catholic-for-life" offspring.

Part of the guilt comes from parents who don't recognize the limits of their power. Nobody can be responsible for another's lifelong faith, not the pope, bishops, or clergy.

Ultimately, all they can do is set a good model and foundation for their children and then trust in God to lead them to him when and in whatever mysterious manner he chooses.

Part of growing up and away from parents involves testing one's beliefs, practices, and values. In *Passages,* Gail Sheehy calls this the "pulling up of roots" stage and explains: "In the attempt to separate our view of the world from our family's view . . . we cast about for any beliefs we can call our own. And in the process of testing those beliefs we are often drawn to fads, preferably those most mysterious and inaccessible to our parents."

Religious disinterest is one of the easiest and quickest fads of separation. The more religion means to the parents, the more likely the separating and maturing adult is to use it as a separating device. Sheehy says of the twenty to thirty-year-olds, "Our backs go up at the merest hint that we are like our parents, that two decades of parental training might be reflected in our current actions and attitudes. 'Not me,' is the motto, 'I'm different.' "

Don't Prejudge Your Child's Faith in God. It's a mistake to view a young adult's disaffection with the church as a lack of interest in God. Many parents write their children off before God does, in fact. While parents are moaning that they have left the church, many young adults view themselves as taking a sabbatical. Like the Prodigal Son, maybe they'll come home someday. Maybe not.

I have three such offspring, ages nineteen, twenty-two, and twenty-six. I know—and they know I know—that they don't attend Mass every Sunday. But we also know it doesn't mean they've turned away from God or the values my husband and I have tried to teach.

One even unwittingly said to me once in a Sunday phone call from college, "I went to church today."

I didn't respond, "Of course, you did. It's Sunday. Don't you go every Sunday?"

Instead, I said, "Good for you. So did we. Was it a good Mass?"

I agree with Thomas Groome and John Westerhoff III who hold that testing a childhood faith is essential if Christians are to adopt an eventual mature adult faith of their own. Westerhoff claims that to reach an "owned" level of faith one must go through the "searching" level—testing one's childhood beliefs and examining alternatives. The prized "owned" faith is a faith that says, "Yes, I believe this, not because Mom and Dad say so or the church says so or I'll go to hell if I don't, but because I really believe."

To get to this level of faith, many (not all) must search. The usual searching years take place between the ages of eighteen and twenty-eight. These are the years that young adults are on their own for the first time and free to test, adopt, or reject parental beliefs and values.

Loving Kids Who Reject the Faith

The love of God for his children is a model of the love parents must have for their children, especially as they get older. He invites us, affirms us, helps us, but never violates the full freedom of our personal choice. His dependable love never forces us, but gently draws us.

We can model faith for our kids. We can give them a good family experience. We can teach them doctrine and take them to church. We can challenge them. But we cannot keep any one of them in a church which they finally choose to reject.

When older children refuse to follow our direction, we can only acquiesce in their decision, while letting them know we disagree. However, we are not left without recourse,

Don't Drive Your Adult Children Away. During these years we parents must be very careful *not* to drive our children permanently away by our questions, nagging, and anger. One mother of six saw all her children abandon the church for a while only to re-enter one by one. "I still have the teeth marks on my tongue," she said. "But I knew their values were good, and they saw me remain constant during their time away. We just never talked about their faith life."

Contrast her with the father who accused his children of wasting his hard-earned money on their Catholic education when they stopped attending Mass. His constant haranguing estranged his children from both him and his church.

A charismatic preacher once said that God knows no grandchildren, referring to the idea that adults do not develop a faith through their parents but through a personal relationship with God. Parents can get in the way of that relationship by implying, "You must believe and practice as I do. Everything else is wrong." When this happens, ma-

continued on next page

since we can intercede for them with prayer and fasting.

God in his mysterious way of loving seems to allow all his children, including parents, to make mistakes. He is trusting beyond our understanding. His love is constant. His mercy keeps open the door to forgiveness and reconciliation. He sees beyond external rejection right into the heart of his children. If we let him, he will bring each of us home. He will give our children many opportunities to come to know and love him, just as he did for us. But they *must choose.* We can only hope and pray.

A wonderful Catholic mother, who has suffered much physical and emotional pain in her family, says with real wisdom, "When they bury me, please put on my headstone 'It didn't turn out the way I planned, but it's okay.'"

Robert R. Iatesta

turity in faith can be stunted.

I grew up with what I now consider a rather superstitious level of faith, which included the nine First Fridays, thirty-day Novenas, and the like. I cannot accept this kind of faith today. I appreciate, however, the witness and depth of my parents' faith that sustained me as I was searching for my own. My children are likely to do the same.

Remaining steadfast in faith while children grow away from it is crucial to both parents' and children's well-being.

They are more involved in addressing injustice, social issues, and peace than I was at their age. On a blustery Christmas Eve last December, we worked in the Catholic Worker Soup Kitchen here in Denver. My nineteen-year-old took off his $40 Reeboks and gave them to a street person who had flapping soles on his wet canvas shoes. Someone scoffed later, "He probably sold them for a bottle of wine."

"So?" my son replied.

Other parents report similar behaviors. "My thirty-year-old and his wife are very active in their church," one said to me. "It hurts that it's not our church; but when I see how strong their faith is, I'm happy for them. My husband and I never shared that kind of spirituality."

Parents don't know why some children in a family reject the church of their childhood while others embrace it. It certainly deflates the idea that the parents failed in establishing a strong spiritual foundation. Perhaps it's God's way of healing the scandal of religious division among his denominations. When we parents see our children finding a deeper faith life outside the Catholic church, it forces us to recognize that we don't have the only road to heaven.

Perhaps it's to show us that beyond a certain age, parents

no longer own their children's wills and lives, that they aren't as powerful as they would like to be, and that parents have to learn to trust in God's direction in their own lives.

Your Catholic Faith Must Remain Strong. Remaining steadfast in faith while children grow away from it is crucial to both parents' and children's well-being. If we parents allow their disaffection to shake our faith, it tells our kids that we practiced spirituality more for their sake than ours.

Abigail McCarthy noted that although her children left the church, they would be appalled if she did because Catholicism is such a deep part of her very being. Wise insight. Testing and straying are much safer when there are solid models at home.

Some grown children return to the church when they have children of their own, but parents can't count on it. They must be able to accept the possibility that their grown children will never return home to Catholicism. It is painful to see grandchildren baptized or confirmed in another church. What's worse is to watch them grow up without any spiritual dimension at all.

I know a grandmother who baptized her new grandchild in the kitchen sink when the parents were gone because she couldn't bear the thought of the baby not being Catholic. Since infant baptism is an offshoot of the parents' faith, the gesture was theologically questionable. But it met the grandmother's needs. She reasoned that because she had failed with her daughter she might somehow save her grandchild.

I wonder how often our concerns for our children's welfare are really ways of fulfilling our own needs fueled by guilt, doubt, failure, and rejection. We parents feel personally rejected when our children reject what we have taught them. We feel as if we have failed as parents if they don't finish school or stay in the church.

Our failure is not with our children but with ourselves and our inability to let go and trust in God. ∎

What Kept Our Kids Catholic

What one family did right—
love, prayer, faith, and fun.

Van and Janet Vandagriff

"Why have your kids remained Catholic?"—that question seemed easy enough to answer until we tried to get specific. When we realized that we really didn't know, we asked our seven children to tell us themselves. The answers were interesting and varied. Here is a sample of some of the responses we got from our children, ages nineteen to thirty-three:

- "The church was not just a *segment* of our lives, but something that was a part of all aspects of what we did as a family."
- "A perception of Mary and the angels and the saints as *real people* instead of just someone to learn about—real people who had an impact on *today*, not just back in biblical times."
- "Our participation in the life of the church—being involved in Mass, in parish life, in CCD and First Communion, in baptisms and confirmation as a *family*, celebrating together instead of just taking part in a series of isolated rituals."
- "Praying together as a family and talking about God and Jesus. Thanking him for our many blessings, and taking problems to him both individually and as a

family as we went through different stages in our lives made him very real."

- "There were so many fun things built around life in the church—brunches after Mass with family and friends, family get-togethers before and after Mass, a lot of serving in the parish. And it wasn't just Mom and Dad, but all the children, too, as each of us got to be old enough."

- "Dad became a Catholic, so I figured there must be something to it."

As we said, the answers were varied, but there seemed to be some common threads running through them.

We tried to show respect for church authority, even in instances where we did not necessarily agree with a particular decision or approach.

Respect for Authority. Our children have developed a respect for the unity and authority of the Catholic church, which we think may have been strongly influenced by the unity they saw in our family. They also felt supported as a result of having a "chain of command" and a respect for authority within our family structure.

As parents we tried to show respect for church authority, even in instances where we did not necessarily agree with a particular decision or approach. Our response in such situations was to freely express our area of disagreement, explain why we felt the way we did, and then emphasize the necessity for obedience in spite of our disagreement.

Our practice of striving to be one in heart and mind as husband and wife was a lesson for our children in the strength of unity. We think the unity of our marriage shaped their attitudes toward church unity.

Fostering an Attitude of Service. Service is another area that had a strong impact on our children as they were growing up in the church. We worked hard to put them to work—in music ministry, as altar boys, setting up chairs for meetings, running the sound system for various church functions, helping with CCD and confirmation programs, and so on. We found that if they were serving, they were more invested in the success of the group or activity, and so were more invested in the church.

Although we tried to see that our children associated mostly with other Christians, particularly in their social lives, we did not try to limit their contacts to Catholics. We have seen good fruit come from this approach. Our children have maintained their love for the Catholic church, while gaining a respect for other Christian denominations. They have many close personal friends who are not Catholic, but have found no reason to be drawn out of the Catholic church into any other denomination.

An Active Social Life. Our vigorous social life with other families was a key factor in our efforts to see that our children did not fall into the traps abounding in our secular society. We would like to be able to claim that we had a master plan for how to accomplish this, but we must admit that much of it just happened. The key was that we simply had fun together as a family, and we enjoyed a major portion of those good times in the company of other Christians.

During the crucial teenage years, our children were more likely to choose to take part in a family get-together or a social event with other Christians instead of going to a high-school-sponsored party. And they did this with little or no pressure from us. It was a matter of attraction rather than coercion.

We think our kids are Catholic today because they met Jesus in our family life— in our prayer, in our fun, in our work, in our play.

During our children's formative years, we frequently welcomed priests and nuns into our home, which gave our children many opportunities to relate to them informally and to get to know them personally. This contributed to our children's respect and admiration for church leaders and bolstered their faith in the Catholic church.

Later, as our children began to move toward marriage decisions, we did not pressure them to consider marrying Catholics. However, we did point out that there are often tensions involved in interfaith marriages. They understood there would be significant issues to resolve should they marry someone from another Christian background.

Introducing Our Kids to Jesus. Beneath all this, we think our kids are Catholic today because they met Jesus in our family life. In our prayer, in our fun, in our work, in our play—he was present, and we helped our kids to see him and know him. One of my (Van's) most vivid memories of how much Jesus was a part of our children's everyday lives stems from a terrifying experience on a dark winter morning. Mary, our eldest daughter was hit by a car as she crossed a busy street to catch a school bus. After I had made sure she wasn't seriously injured, I heard from some of the other young people at the bus stop about her strong witness of faith. When Mary was hit by the car—as she was flying through the air—she didn't scream. She simply said, "Praise the Lord!" I recall thinking at the time just how far ahead of me some of my children were in their relationship with Jesus!

Lest we give the impression that our life was a cross between the Brady Bunch and Father Knows Best, we want to make it clear that we had to deal with some very serious problems, including rebellion, drugs, alcohol, and other menacing situations that all parents seem to face in today's world.

Seeking God's Help. Very early on as our older children got into their teen years, we came to realize that we simply didn't have what it took to raise children in this world with all its challenges. At that point we went to our knees and asked God to take care of them. We offered to try to hear his voice and discern his will in raising our children.

Since that time, we have seen God work miracles in their lives as they went through the various stages of growing to maturity. We have seen four of them marry good, strong Christians and continue to live a Christian life in the Catholic church. They are raising our fifteen grandchildren, and they have the support of other concerned Catholic families.

We try to do our part, too. Janet regularly prays a rosary for all of our children and grandchildren, and Van tries to submit his will to the wisdom of God when he must make decisions regarding the children. It seems to be a never-ending (and sometimes impossible) task, but God has consistently honored his promise to us regarding our children. We can only seek his mercy and forgiveness for the many times we have failed to uphold our end of the bargain—only to get up, start afresh and "keep on keeping on." ∎

With Faith, Hope, and Love

These virtues have practical consequences for raising Catholic families, and they sum up the key advice of **Keeping Your Kids Catholic.**

Bert Ghezzi

When we look at each of our seven children and let the complexities of raising them sink in, Mary Lou and I feel like beginners, still learning the business we've been in for half of our lives. Undeniably, raising kids Catholic is hard work. Yet, when we're feeling the pressure—applied masterfully by a sixteen-year-old expert in outmaneuvering us in family politics—we try to remind ourselves that there is *Someone* who's even more interested than we in our kids' salvation.

As I emphasized in the opening article of *Keeping Your Kids Catholic,* the real work of bringing families to Christ is God's, and he wants it even more than we do. All we can do is appeal to our children's hearts. It's up to the Holy Spirit to win their hearts. That is why Mary Lou and I work as though everything depended on us, knowing that everything actually depends on him and that he's at work even when we cannot see it.

God helps us in raising our children as Catholics by giving us powerful graces. Among these are the traditional virtues of faith, hope, and love. Sometimes called the theological virtues, they have very practical implications for our family life. Many writers of *Keeping Your Kids Catholic* have already discussed elements of faith, hope, and love. Here's a summary of their important roles:

- **Faith.** We *believe* that the Lord wants to draw our kids to himself. This faith releases the grace and power of God—the Holy Spirit—for the daily tasks of family building that we feel too weak and inadequate to accomplish on our own.

- **Hope.** No, we don't often get immediate results, but we *expect* that God will ultimately win our children. We're not talking here about that flimsy notion of hope current in such expressions as "I hope so." That kind of hope is merely a wish that evaporates as soon as troubles come. Our hope is the sturdy, reliable kind because it anchors us in God. We can count on him to save our children, because he already gave up his own child for that very purpose.

- **Love.** The virtue of love also has obvious practical applications for raising our kids Catholic. First, we must love our kids no matter what. Second, we must love God wholeheartedly. Aiming our love in these two directions will help us stay on target in building strong Catholic families.

Growing up is tough, and our children need us every step of the way. That means standing by them for a quarter of a century or more, supporting them in whatever way we can—from everyday successes or failures to major life choices, celebrations, or crises.

Over the years we must learn to tailor our love to fit their changing needs, so that they can feel in their bones that we are with them. Mary Lou and I try to focus our love by asking, "What is the loving thing to do for this child now?" The answer may be to laugh with them or to cry with them, to say no when they wanted yes, to affirm or to upbraid them, to let them become independent or to let them depend on us when they need to.

Loving our children also means letting them make their own faith decisions as they grow older. Religious educators tell us now what we should have surmised from our own experience: it is common for adolescents to question faith, doubt religious truth, and criticize traditions.

Parents must say and do a lot to introduce their children to the Lord and to the church. Our influence is an essential part of the process that brings them to faith. But searching

---

If we want to keep our kids Catholic, then we must be good Catholics ourselves.

---

can be a healthy way for youths to come to an adult commitment. We must be patient, bearing with them through the sulkiness and negativity that may crop up during their teen years, so that we can assist them in finding the relationship with God that they are searching for. I always try to look at the dark, brooding side of our teenagers' moods as a promise of their spiritual awakening, the messy underside of a wonderful, intricate tapestry soon to be revealed.

Being Good Catholics Ourselves. What we are seems to be even more important than what we do in the business of raising Catholic children. If we want to keep our kids Catholic, then we must be good Catholics ourselves. Do you want your children to love God with their whole heart, their whole mind, and their whole strength? Then you must love God in just that way yourself. There's no way around it. You cannot expect your children to embrace God and his church if you have kept him at arm's length. If you have not given yourself to God, you have not taken the first step to keeping your kids Catholic. Why wait another day?

It would be nice to be able to conclude this book with a money-back guarantee that if you do as directed your kids will automatically grow up to become adult Catholics. That guarantee, however, is not mine to give. There's no formula, no magic, no "seven easy steps." While Mary Lou and I have applied much of the advice given in *Keeping Your Kids Catholic* for twenty-five years, we are not yet about to judge how well it has worked for us.

Sometimes, however, we get inklings that reassure us. On our twenty-fifth wedding anniversary, our children presented us with a book containing "love letters" from each of them. The four oldest independently told us how much our love for the family and our love for God influenced them personally in accepting our values. That may not have signaled victory, but it sure indicated progress. I pray that when you get far enough along to look back, you will be able to say at least the same and perhaps much more. ∎

Think, Pray, & Act

HOW ARE WE DOING?

FOR REFLECTION AND DISCUSSION

1. If your child leaves the church, what is your responsibility? (See articles by Curran and Iatesta.)
2. What seem to be the most important things parents can do to draw their kids close to God and keep them Catholic? (See articles by the Vandagriffs, Lauer, and Ghezzi.)
3. In your opinion, what is the single most important thing a parent can do to raise a child Catholic?

TAKING STOCK

Are you wondering if you are doing any better at keeping your kids Catholic? Answer the following questions, which you answered earlier, to help assess your progress:

1. Am I the kind of Catholic I want my children to become?
2. Do my faith and my behavior show my children how to live as Catholic Christians? If asked, would my children say I did what I told them to do?
3. What goals do I have for my children?
4. Is loving God and putting God first in life a top priority for me? Have I made it a top priority for my children?
5. Take an inventory of Catholic practices in your family:
    —family prayer (at meals, before bedtime, other)
    —read Scripture or Catholic books to the family
    —have special meal on Sunday (brunch or dinner)
    —make Sunday special by doing something as a
      family
    —worship together at Mass on Sunday

—subscribe to Catholic magazines and have Catholic books
—celebrate seasons and Christian holidays
—celebrate in a special way birthdays, baptisms, First Communion, confirmation and so on
—make use of parish programs such as religious education
—decorate with Catholic Christian art
—teach the children Catholic prayers, such as the rosary, and use them as a family
—other (specify)

6. If you have introduced some of these practices, which seem to be working well? Which don't seem to work?

Now turn to **Taking Stock** for chapters three and chapter four.

• Compare today's answers to your earlier ones.
• What signs of progress do you see?
• What area do you need to work on the most?

PLAN FOR ACTION

1. Review your decisions about personal prayer and family prayer. If you have not implemented them or if for some reason you have stopped doing them, try again.
2. Consider the area you think you must work on the most. Is there a single, simple decision you could make which would bring a big improvement? Review the parts of *Keeping Your Kids Catholic* that pertain to the area. What else should you do to help your family in this area?

ACTIVITY

Have another family fun night. (See **Activity** for chapter five. If you have not tried this event, consider doing one soon.)

Copyright Acknowledgments

227

Keeping Your Kids Catholic Workshop

A Workshop of Study, Prayer, and Hope
For Dads and Moms
And For Everyone Who Loves Kids

Presented by Bert Ghezzi

- **Talks** Offering Real Help and Hope
- **Answers** to Your Questions and Solutions That Work
- **Discussions** with Others Who Share Your Concerns
- **Prayer** for Parents and Their Children

The *Keeping Your Kids Catholic* WORKSHOP can be adapted easily to fit the special circumstances of parishes or groups. For more information about the workshop and about how you can sponsor one in your area, write to

Bert Ghezzi
Keeping Your Kids Catholic Workshop
P.O. Box 1902
Winter Park, FL 32790-1902